MUSIC IN YOUR CLASSROOM
An Activities Program for Music Skills, Appreciation, and Creativity

MUSIC IN YOUR CLASSROOM
An Activities Program for Music Skills, Appreciation, and Creativity

Ruth Zinar, Ph.D.

PARKER PUBLISHING COMPANY, INC.
WEST NYACK, NEW YORK

© 1983 by

PARKER PUBLISHING COMPANY, INC.

West Nyack, NY

Library of Congress Cataloging in Publication Data

Zinar, Ruth
  Music in your classroom.

  Includes index.
  1. Music—Instruction and study—Juvenile.   2. Games
with music.   I. Title.
MT742.Z56   1983   372.8'7044   82-22351
ISBN 0-13-606954-1

Printed in the United States of America

This book is dedicated—

To the memory of my parents, with gratitude,
To Milton, Susan, Gail, and Larry, with love,
and
To Michelle and all of her generation, with hope.

Introduction

There are many things that can be done with music—even by someone who knows little about it. It is not necessary to be a trained musician to bring some of the joy, the beauty, and the values of music to the classroom through the games and activities described in this book.

Here, classroom teachers—as well as elementary school music educators—will find step-by-step instructions for helping their pupils to respond to melody and rhythm, learn basic rudiments of music, and to express their musical impulses freely, originally, and creatively.

These activities involve many aspects of music. There are games and enjoyable exercises for use in teaching note reading, rhythmic notation, ear training, music appreciation lessons, and for developing the child's musical creativity and sense of rhythm and pitch acuity. They include games using body movement for self-expression and for learning music facts, rhythm band activities, singing, pencil and paper games, group games, art, dramatization and listening.

In addition, because the handicapped child can participate in many simple music activities (what he can't understand he can still enjoy), where appropriate, suggestions are given for specific activities or for variations on the games and the techniques to make them suitable for the child who has been mainstreamed.

Most of the ideas presented in this book require only a limited knowledge of music. No one need feel that he cannot use music because he has had little or no musical background, or has no "talent," or is "tone-deaf," or "can't sing on pitch." Indeed, you can learn the basic rudiments and develop your own musicality while presenting the activity to the class, and the clear, simple, step-by-step directions can help the classroom teacher who is not musically inclined get pupils musically and actively involved.

On the other hand, if you are an experienced, talented, knowledgeable, and trained music teacher, you will find in this book an organized compendium of ideas for teaching music at various grade and ability levels and in various classroom situations, that will help to expand and vary your repertoire of music activities and games.

These techniques, suggestions, and ideas can do much on a day-to-day basis to help you understand that music is not only a most enjoyable part of the curriculum to which all children look forward, but also that it serves as an effective outlet which can change an undesirable tone of a class to one of peace and harmony. We all know the power of music to affect mood—to arouse children when they are lethargic, to soothe them when they are tense or overexcited, and to provide physical release for pent-up energy.

There is music in the world about us, in the acceleration and slowing down of a train, the grinding of a machine, the clip-clop of a horse's hooves, the songs of birds. Little children can feel these things, but unless this feeling is developed, it is frequently suppressed and hidden in the course of growing up.

The joy of music shared through this book can do much to help you reach your students, using music frequently and in many ways. And what is more, you will find your school days and your school life made richer and more enjoyable by the music you bring to your classes.

RZ

Acknowledgments

Many thanks to Willet Ryder for providing
the illustrations that appear in this book.

Contents

Developing
the Sense of Pitch

BODY MOVEMENT

In all of the following games and activities in which body movements respond to high and low pitch, the best instrument to use would be the Melody Bells (also called Song Bells). These are not really bells, but rather, an instrument made up of a series of tuned metal bars which are mounted on a wooden frame. The black and white bars are arranged to look like the piano keyboard and they are struck with a mallet. Each bar has the name of its tone indicated on it with the lowest tone on the left side and the highest on the right. (See illustration.)

By holding the instrument vertically, with the lowest tones at the bottom, it can become, visually as well as aurally, a "music ladder." Then, as the children *hear* the sound of rising and falling pitch, they can *see* the low and high bars being struck, and *feel* the responses of their bodies moving up and down with the pitch.

Another useful classroom instrument is an inexpensive set of Swiss Melody Bells. These *do* look like and are played like bells. Each one is a different color and has the name of the tone indicated. The advantages of this instrument are its flexibility and sweet tones. One child can play a tune on all of the bells or as many as are needed can be distributed among several children. Or else a few (e.g.: c, e, g) can be rung together to sound lovely chords and form a harmony for simple songs.

When using the melody bells to develop the sense of pitch, it is a good idea to make each activity gradually more challenging. At first, the pupils watch as you play the vertically held bells, raising and lowering their arms or bodies as the pitch goes up and down. Play the tones at random—some close together, some with large intervals (spaces) between them. Then, place the bells horizontally on a table and have the children try to follow the higher and lower pitches. Finally, with eyes closed so that they are working independently, the children move their arms or bodies up and down with the changing pitch.

Do not expect the body or arm response to the changing pitch to be accurate after one or two tries. A few minutes several times a week for many weeks—or months—of practice may be needed to develop this skill. That is why it is important to approach this activity through various games and in many imaginative ways.

The basic idea is the same for the next few games which are suitable for younger children. They see and hear you play ascending and descending tones on the vertically held melody bells. Squatting low for the low tones, they gradually rise as the tones ascend, until they stand erect with arms upraised. As descending tones are played, they gradually return to a squatting position. Each time you do this activity, the children can "be" something else.

Going Up and Down Games

Rising and Setting Sun

Starting close to the ground with their eyes closed and heads in arms, the children are "suns." As the ascending tones are played, they open their eyes and stand a little at a time. As the highest tone is reached, their raised arms encircle their heads. Then, as the tones go lower, they are "setting suns," gradually returning to their original positions, arms again covering their heads and eyes closed once more.

Going Up and Down the Stairs

This time, the children bend low to start but as they "go up" or "go down" the stairs with the rising and falling pitch, they pump their legs up and down to imitate climbing up and down steps.

Riding the Elevator

The movement this time is more rapid and smooth. As they start raising their bodies, the children call out, "Going up!" with rising inflection. As they start down, they chant, "Going down!"

Climbing Up and Down the Mountains

In this game, the hands and arms are used in climbing motion as the children "climb up the mountain" to rising pitch or "down the mountain" to falling pitch.

Use Body Position to Indicate Pitch

Make the children agree that their heads are their highest part, their feet, the lowest. Therefore, when you sing in a high voice they will wash their faces; when you sing in a low voice, they will put on their socks. As you sing in a high, "squeaky" voice to "The Farmer in the Dell,"

> You wash your face today,
> You wash your face today,
> Hi-ho, the derry-oh,
> You wash your face today ... ,

the children pretend to wash their faces. When you sing in a low, "growly" voice, "Put on your socks today ... ," the children put on their socks.

After the children have done this activity once or twice, repeat. But this time, change the tone of voice as you change from one verse to another:

> You wash your face today, (high voice)
> Put on your socks today, (low voice)
> Hi-ho, the derry-oh, (high voice)
> Put on your socks today. (low voice)

As the voice quality changes, the children's motions should change. Keep them guessing when you will change.

To evaluate their ability to recognize high and low pitch, have them all close their eyes so that they cannot imitate their classmates. Then sing the tune without words, changing frequently from high to low pitch, and watch to see how many children are able to respond correctly.

Tiptoe and Bend Low

If you can play the piano or a melody on the bells, do so; otherwise, just play any very low tones. The children stand and as the low tones are played, they walk around, bent low towards the ground. Change to high tones and the children walk on tiptoe with arms held high. As you change back and forth from high to low tones, varying the amount of time for each, the children respond by either bending low or walking on their toes.

Be Giants or Dwarfs

This game is similar, but children pretend to be someone else. As low or high tones are played on the piano or the melody bells, the children vary their walking posture—squatting close to the ground as they walk like dwarfs, or on their toes, reaching upwards with arms outstretched and taking large steps, as they walk like giants.

Play Sliding Pond

Children squat low, close to the ground. The teacher plays ascending tones on the melody bells and children "climb the ladder," going higher and higher until they are standing on their toes, stretching arms up to the sky. Then, as the teacher suddenly plays the lowest tone on the melody bells, the children quickly go down the "slide" to the floor. Repeat this several times, each time going a different distance up the ladder or remaining at the top of the slide for different lengths of time; add the element of surprise.

Repeat, this time having the children keep their eyes closed so that you can see if they can really hear the changes or if they are imitating each other.

Be a Jack-in-the-Box

The children squat low and stay close to the ground as the teacher plays a whole series of low tones on the melody bells. Then, as a high tone is suddenly played, they jump up high, clapping their hands over their heads. Repeat this several times, varying the length of time the low tones are played so that there is always the element of surprise.

Wave Scarves

Distribute several colorful scarves. As high-pitched tones are played, the children move (or dance), waving the scarves high in the air. As low tones are played, scarves are waved close to the ground. Vary the pitch.

Take Turns Moving to Changing Pitch

Divide the class into three groups—High, Middle, and Low. As high-pitched melodies are played on the piano or melody bells, or appropriate recordings are played, those children who are in the High group move or dance to the music. When the music is changed to a low or middle register, the children in the High group "freeze," remaining in the position in which they were when the music changed, and those children move who represent the register of the new music. Vary the music so that the groups take turns dancing or remaining motionless. This activity is suitable for pupils in all elementary school grades.

Touch the Pitch Position

Play an ascending scale (which can be represented by the white bars of the melody bells from one C to the C an octave above). As you do this, the children touch the portion of their bodies that corresponds to the tone being played. Then go down the scale as the children reverse the order in which they touch the appropriate parts of their bodies.

This activity is suitable for all grade levels.

C — toes	F — waist	B — ears
D — knees	G — chest	C — top of head
E — hips	A — neck	

Find the Correct Pitch Position

This activity is more difficult than any of the preceding ones and should be done only after the others no longer represent a challenge. Play the scale tones in any order (ending on the lower C) and see if any of the children can guess on which portion of their bodies they should place their hands. Expect only an approximate response. (If any of the children seem to be correct most of or all of the time, it is possible that they have exceptionally good ears for pitch—perhaps, even what is known as "absolute pitch.")

Move with the Song

As children sing a familiar song, have them move their bodies up and down to indicate the rise and fall of the melody, as illustrated on page 20.

Twink- le,   twink- le,   lit- tle

star...

Sing with Arm Movements

Have the class sing a familiar song, especially noting the rise and fall of the melody. Have them repeat it slowly, this time raising and lowering their arms as the melodic pitch rises and falls.

BODY MOVEMENT FOR INTERMEDIATE GRADES

All pupils can benefit from body response to high and low pitch. Children in grades 4-6, however, may feel silly playing such games as "Sliding Pond" or "Giants and Dwarfs." There are activities that are more appropriate for their age level and can get them involved in moving to high and low sounds. The following games and activities are also appropriate for situations in which, for some reason, whole body movements are limited because of physical disabilities.

Catch High and Low Balls

Explain to the class that ball players have to practice in order to be able to play well, and it is necessary to practice to hear music well. In this game, they will practice "catching" musical "high and low balls." Play a low tone on the melody bells. Pupils reach down and clasp their hands to catch a low ball. Play a high tone, and they jump (or reach) high to catch a fly ball. Vary the pitch of the tones played as they practice catching the ball at different levels.

Raise and Lower the Flag

In response to ascending tones played on melody bells, the pupils "raise the flag." Starting close to the floor, they raise hand over hand, going higher and higher as they pretend to pull on a rope. When the highest note is reached, they salute; then they "lower the flag" as the notes descend.

Sit and Stand

Children stand as high tones are played, sit as low tones are played.

Ride the Waves

Surfing has strong appeal for older children. They can pretend to be riding the waves. Play sweeping tones up and down the piano or by gliding the mallet up and down the melody bells. The children stand in place and move their arms up and down in wave-like motions according to the direction of the pitch. Then, when the lowest tone on the instrument is suddenly struck, they quickly sit down again.

In case physical disabilities preclude standing and sitting down quickly, the same activity can be done seated. The arms can be waved gently and then placed on top of the desk as the low tone is played.

Move Your Arms to the Sound of the Pitch

The pupils watch as you play the vertically held melody bells, raising and lowering their arms as the pitch goes up and down. Play the tones at random—some close together, some with larger intervals between them. Use both white and black bars. Then, as the bells are placed in horizontal position and played that way, the pupils try to follow the higher and lower pitches with their arms. Finally, with eyes closed, they move their arms up and down with the changing pitch.

THE VOICE

Imitate Sounds; Play Follow the Leader (Suitable for early childhood classes)

Train Whistles

Tell the children that you will make sounds like a train whistle and that they are then to make the same sound. You sing "Toot-toot" on one tone; they imitate. Sing again, on a different tone; they imitate. Keep repeating, always on different tones.

Fog-Horns

This time, the children will pretend to be fog-horns. Sing a sustained tone ("Oo---ooh"). The children imitate. Sing again on a lower tone; again they imitate. Repeat on various tones.

Fire Sirens

Imitate fire sirens. As voices go up and down, singing "Ee---ee-eeh!" hands go up and down with the pitch.

Wind

Have the children do the same thing, this time raising and lowering their arms as they sing "Oo-----oh" in ascending and descending pitch in imitation of the sound of wind.

Sing the Roll Call

Sing the child's name and have him or her answer you singing the same tones. Use the tones which make up the "universal children's chant:"

The child answers:

Give each child a chance to reply to his or her name.

Another time, as you sing the question, move your hand up and down to show the direction of the pitch. Have the children follow the movements whenever they want to.

Sing Echoes (Suitable for all age groups)

Make up little fragments of melody and have the class sing them back to you. Any tune you sing will be all right—it's *your melody.* The words should be appropriate for the age and grade of the children in the class.

Hel - lo—   How are you?   Come and play—

Won't you play   to - day?   Yoo - hoo! (etc.)

Compose an Echo

Have a child be the "composer," singing any short phrase he can create. The class echoes the song.

Sing Songs with Hand Movement

When teaching a song, move your hands up and down to show the direction of the pitch. Encourage the pupils to imitate your hand movements.

Combine Voice and Body Movement

Occasionally, teach a song such as the one following. Have the children move their bodies up and down to follow the meaning of the words and the pitch of the melody.

SWINGING SONG

RUTH ZINAR

In a moderate tempo

Won't   you   come   and   swing   with   me?   Won't   you   come   and

sing   with   me?   First   swing   up,   up,   up   high.   Then

down   we'll   go,   by   and   by.   Up   and   up,   then

up   we'll   go,   Quick - ly   go   down,   down   so   low.

Sing Echo Songs

"Ol' Texas" is a favorite cowboy song which is sung as an echo song. The same sort of echo effect can be used in the French folk song, "Frère Jacques." One half of the class sings the first phrase, and then the other half of the class repeats it softly. This is done throughout the song.

OL' TEXAS

COWBOY SONG

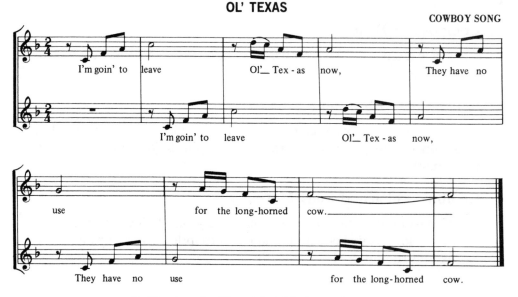

2. They've plow'd and fenc'd my cattle range,
   And the people there are all so strange.

3. I'll bid good-bye to the Alamo,
   And set my face toward Mexico.

FRÈRE JACQUES

FRENCH FOLK SONG

PAPER AND PENCIL ACTIVITIES

Match Pictures with High and Low Pitch

Distribute pictures of people or things which make high or low sounds (e.g.: for high sounds: a flute, a mouse, a bird, a woman singing, a baby, a whistle, "jingle bells," a violin; for low sounds: a man singing, a bear, a lion, a church bell, a tuba, a bullfrog, a double bass). On one part of the chalkboard, write the word "HIGH"; on another part, write "LOW."

One by one, name the objects in the pictures. The child holding the named picture comes to the front of the room and stands in front of the appropriate word. When all the children holding pictures are at the front of the room, the teacher or another child acts as the conductor, alternately holding up signs saying "High" or "Low." The children holding pictures which belong to the indicated category imitate the sounds made by the objects in their pictures.

As the conductor changes the indications from high to low, the sounds should change accordingly.

Make a Sound Chart

Have two large poster-size sheets of oaktag. On one, print the words "High Sounds"; on the other, "Low Sounds." Have the children bring in or draw pictures of things that make high or low sounds and paste them on the appropriate chart.

Follow the Dots

As the teacher slowly plays a short tune on the melody bells, the children draw dots from left to right on a piece of paper, to indicate whether the tones are going up or down. Then, as the melody is played again, they connect the dots, in this way seeing the "contour" —the "shape"—of the melody.

Show the Pitch with Arrows

As fragments of tunes are played in very slow tempo, children draw arrows pointing up and down to show the direction of the pitch.

Way, down u-pon the Swa-nee ri-ver....

Write Circles Up and Down

Each child is given a sheet of paper. The teacher (or one of the children) plays notes at random on the melody bells. Children draw circles on the paper to indicate pitch level—high if the pitch is high, low if the pitch is low, in the middle of the paper if the pitch is in a middle register.

Show Rising and Falling Pitch with Stick Figures

Provide each child with a worksheet showing "hills." Play a series of tones on the melody bells. If the sound goes up, the children draw stick figures going up the hill. If the tones go down, the figures go down. (See the illustration.)

Find High or Low Things

Play a series of tones on the melody bells. If you play high tones, each child writes a list of all the "high" things he can find in the room (e.g., ceiling, light, pictures, clock, etc.). If you play low tones, things found close to the floor are listed (e.g.: children's feet, shoes, floor, etc.). If tones are played in the middle register, the list might include desks, table, windowsill, doorknob, etc.

Children change papers and mark each other's work for spelling, accuracy in recognizing pitch, and accuracy in placing the object listed as high or low.

Mainstreamed children who have too much difficulty in keeping up with the rest of the class in finding and listing objects can take turns being the ones to play the tones on the melody bells.

Place Circles on Pictures to Indicate Pitch

Distribute worksheets using pictures similar to the following:

1. A picture showing a country scene with flowers, cows, grass, trees, sky, birds.
2. A picture of a city street with cars, fire hydrant, buildings, chimneys, clouds in the sky, street lamp.

3. A picture of a bridge over a river, boat in the river, bus on the bridge, rocket in the sky.

Play a tone on the melody bells and have the children draw a circle on that part of the picture which would indicate the pitch level. Repeat, playing various pitch levels as the children draw the circles (e.g., circle on the rocket for a high tone, on the river for a low tone, on the bus for a middle tone).

Show the Pitch on the Ladder

Children receive work sheets showing a ladder with eight rungs. As tones of the scale (i.e.: white bars from one C to another) are played, they draw circles on the rungs. This can be done to show either ascending or descending tones. (See the illustration.)

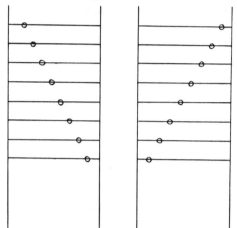

See the Melody Move

Prepare a transparency on which is placed the title of a familiar song. As the class sings the song, draw curved lines representing the rise and fall of the melody on the transparency. In this way, the pupils can see the melody "move" as they sing.

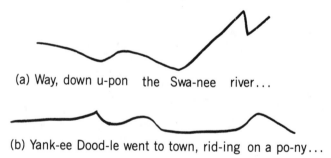

(a) Way, down u-pon   the Swa-nee   river...

(b) Yank-ee Dood-le went to town, rid-ing on a po-ny...

Identify the Register of the Melody

Prepare a chart with three columns labeled "High," "Medium," and "Low," as illustrated.

Play a series of melodic fragments on the piano or melody bells in different registers (levels of pitch)—some high, some low, some in a middle register. Have the children place a check in the correct column

	HIGH	MIDDLE	LOW
1.			
2.			
3.			
4.			
5.			
	etc.		

for each fragment. Replay the fragments and have them discuss what they hear and decide the pitch level, checking to see how many correct answers they had.

Develop Your Pitch Memory

Prepare worksheets as illustrated.

	SAME	DIFFERENT
1.		
2.		
3.		
4.		
5.		

As the pupils listen carefully, play a melodic fragment of three tones. Play it again—either repeating it exactly or changing one tone. The pupils decide whether the second tune was the same as or different from the first and place a check in the appropriate column. Replay the fragments and have the class discuss them, deciding whether they were the same or different as they check their papers.

When, after practicing over a period of time, the children have developed skill in recognizing melodic repetition or change, gradually increase the length of the melodies played. You may want to change more than one tone of the melody.

Identify the Register of Sound in the Environment

Take your class for a walk and have them listen to the sounds around them. In a park, they might hear children playing, mothers calling, birds singing, pigeons cooing, a peanut vendor's whistle squealing, a dog barking, or people talking. Walking on a city street, they might hear radios or cassette players playing, cars starting, horns blowing, motors turning, people talking. Have them list all the sounds they can hear and identify the register of each. Have them decide whether the sound has a definite pitch or is just a "noise."

Match the Tune with Its Contour

Prepare worksheets showing two columns. In one column, list titles of very familiar tunes. In the other column, in different order, have diagrams of the melodic contours of these tunes. Children are to match the tune with its contour. Select songs that vary considerably in melodic contour. This activity is suitable for children in upper elementary grades. (See the illustration.)

ANSWER	SONG TITLE	MELODIC CONTOUR
e	1. Joy to the World	a.
c	2. Hot Cross Buns	b.
b	3. Swanee River	c.
a	4. Twinkle, Twinkle, Little Star	d.
d	5. Home on the Range	e.

Next to each number, write the letter of the melodic contour that describes the melody.

MISCELLANEOUS ACTIVITIES

Find the High and the Low Bells

Distribute Swiss Melody Bells at random to a number of children in the room. Have them take turns playing the bells while the rest of the class decides which are higher and which are lower in sound. Then see if those who have the bells can play them, one at a time, in ascending order.

Find the Highest and the Lowest Bells

Place any five bells on a table in random order. One child plays all of them and tries to decide which one is the highest and which one is the lowest in pitch.

Play Echoes

Tell the children to listen and watch closely and then to do what you did. Play a brief fragment of melody on the Swiss Melody Bells. See if any of the children can repeat the same melodic fragment. Start with very brief two-tone melodies. If enough of the children are successful, add another tone and then another, gradually making the tunes a little longer.

Arrange the Swiss Melody Bells

Place the Swiss Melody Bells on a table in "mixed-up" order. The child tries to arrange them in ascending order so that a scale can be played on them.

Play "Mixed-Up" Bells

The mixed-up bells are on the table. Then, eight children are selected to stand alongside each other in front of the room. The child who is "It" gives each one a bell, then keeps rearranging the children holding the bells until they are in the correct order to play a scale. (The child who is hard of hearing can participate by being one of the children holding a bell.)

Find the Matching Tone

This is a more difficult game than the preceding one. "It" comes to the front of the room and plays any tone on the melody bells. Another child tries to "find" the same tone on another melody bell. If he is wrong, "It" repeats the original tone until the other child is able to find the matching tone.

Variation on "Hot and Cold" (Party Game)

This is a variation of the familiar children's party game "Hot and Cold" and it could be used during class parties, recreation periods, etc. "It" goes out of the room and an object is hidden. "It" returns and as he or she tries to find the object and moves closer to it, the tones played on the melody bells (or piano, if possible) get higher and higher. (Use the black notes or "chromatic" tones also.) As "It" moves further from the object, the pitch gets lower and lower. (Hopefully, the object will be found before you run out of tones!)

Use Kodaly Signals

The famous Kodaly signals were not originated by the composer, Zoltan Kodaly. In 1841, John Curwen, a British Congregational minister who was interested in teaching children, was commissioned to find the simplest way of teaching singing by note for use by chorus and in hymn singing. Gradually, he evolved his system (called the "Tonic Sol-Fa Method") which included using a series of hand signals to represent the scale tones (do, re, mi, fa, sol, la, ti, do).

Zoltan Kodaly, the eminent Hungarian composer, later incorporated these signals into his sight singing method. Kodaly's whole approach has been extremely successful and not only is it used throughout Hungary, but many music schools and music teachers in other countries have incorporated its aspects into their own teaching. The game-like use of hand signals has been especially popular.

Although it takes much study and training to become a "Kodaly teacher," the simplest elements of the hand signaling can easily be used by all teachers and they provide an enjoyable, obvious, and extremely valuable way to help to develop pitch sensitivity and the beginnings of sight singing ability. What is more, using the hand signals fascinates pupils of all ages—from early childhood to adulthood.

The following exercises move simply and gradually. Stay with each level until most of the children are singing the tones accurately.

The hand signals for the four tones used in these early exercises are shown in the illustration.

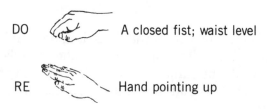

DO   A closed fist; waist level

RE   Hand pointing up

MI 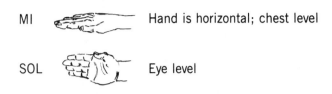 Hand is horizontal; chest level

SOL   Eye level

Follow the Hand Signals: Sing Three Consecutive Tones

Kodaly starts with only two different tones, but because they can be easily learned and because so many familiar tunes can be sung using them, three tones—do, re, mi—are used here.

Using the hand signals for "do, re, mi" (if you do them with two hands, they will be more clearly distinguished), have the children imitate the hand signals as they sing several times:

> do, re, mi;
> mi, re, do.

Sing Three "Mixed-Up" Tones

Start with "do" and then signal the tones "do," "re," and "mi," in any order, as the children imitate the hand gestures and sing what is signaled. At first, sing along to help them. Gradually withdraw your help until they are doing well at singing the three tones.

Sing Tunes on Three Tones Using Kodaly Signals

Here are some well-known tunes using the three tones, "do, re, mi."

Signal them in the correct rhythm:

Hot Cross Buns

> Hot cross buns,
> Mi,   re,   do,
> Hot cross buns,
> Mi,   re,   do,
> One, a penny, two, a penny,
> Do, do,do,do,   re, re,re,re,
> Hot cross buns.
> Mi,   re,   do.

Mary Had a Little Lamb

> Ma-ry had a   lit-tle lamb,
> Mi,re, do,   re, mi,mi, mi

Lit-tle lamb, lit- tle lamb,
Re,re, re,   mi,mi, mi,

Ma-ry had a   lit- tle, lamb,
Mi,re, do,   re, mi,mi, mi

Its fleece was white as snow.
Mi,re,   re, mi,   re, do.

Au Clair de la Lune
("By the Light of the Moon")

Au clair de la lu-ne,
Do,do, do, re, mi,re,

Mon am-i Pierr-ot,
Do, mi,re, re, do,

Pret-ez moi ta plu-me,
Do, do,do, re, mi, re,

Pour é-crire un mot.
Do, mi,re, re, do.

Trolley Song

Ding, ding, ding, went the trol-ley,
Mi,   mi,   mi,   re,   do, re, mi,

Ding, ding, ding, went the bell,
Mi,   mi,   mi,   re,   do, re,

Ding, ding, ding, went my heart-strings,
Mi,   mi,   mi,   re,   do, re,   mi,

For the mo-ment I   saw him, I   fell.
Do, re, mi,do,   re, mi, do, re, do.

Compose a Three-Tone Song Using Kodaly Signals

Choose a volunteer from among the children to compose and lead a three-tone song. The child signals a tune using the gestures for "do," "re," and "mi" in any order while the class sings.

Sing Two More Tones Using Kodaly Signals

The tones used here are "sol" and "mi" (represented on the bells by g and e). Notice that the tune sounds like the childhood chant or call, "Yoo-hoo!" and the bird call, "Cuck-oo." Use the hand signals as children imitate them and sing, "Sol-mi, sol-mi." Repeat this until they are very familiar with the signals and the two tones.

Sing "Mixed-Up" Two Tones

Use the hand signals for "sol" and "mi," this time repeating any of the tones and signaling them in any order. Make up different combinations.

(a) Sol-mi, sol-mi,
Sol, sol, sol, sol,
Sol-mi.

(b) Sol, mi, mi, sol,
Sol, mi, mi, mi,
Mi, sol.

(c) Sol, mi, mi, mi,
Mi--, sol,
Sol, mi, mi, mi
Mi, mi, mi--.

Sing Four Tones Using Kodaly Signals

Now combine "sol-mi" and "mi, re, do." Signal them in groups such as:

(a) Sol-mi, sol-mi, sol-mi,
mi, re, do.

(b) Mi, re, do,
Mi, re, do,
Sol, mi, sol, mi, sol, mi,
Mi, re, do.

Sing Four "Mixed-Up" Tones

Start to signal the four tones used so far in any order at all. Sing along with the class to help. Gradually withdraw your help until they are able to sing the four tones from your signals.

Skill in responding to the Kodaly signals can be developed over a period of time with frequent, short, practice periods.

When the children are able to sing from the hand signals, they will be ready to start to sing the syllables from the two-line and three-line staffs. These Kodaly activities are described in Chapter 2.

Reading Pitch Notation

A NOTE ABOUT NOTES

There are probably millions of people who know that "Every Good Boy Does Fine," and that this mnemonic tells the names of the lines on the staff. Some even know that the notes in the spaces spell the word "FACE." Unfortunately, their knowledge stops there. They have never used this information in any way and the learning is therefore meaningless.

Actually, music notation serves several purposes:

1. It can show whether the *sound* of the tones goes higher or lower or stays on the same pitch.
2. It can show repetition—whether a melodic pattern is repeated or changed.
3. It can show contour—whether the melody moves in a smooth step-by-step manner or skips to another tone. And if the tone skips, music notation can show whether there is a small distance between the tones or a large, more abrupt shift from a lower tone to a higher tone or vice versa.
4. It can tell a performer exactly *which* tones to play, the same notation being used for the most difficult virtuoso or orchestral music and for the simplest classroom music.

All of these functions of notation are explored and taught in the games and activities that follow. Children see, hear, write, play, and move to melodic sounds—sounds that have been transformed and designated by precise symbols.

All aspects are important. For this reason, there are a number of activities that use the simplest of classroom instruments—melody bells and Swiss Melody Bells.

These are especially simple to use because, once the written note is identified, the name can be found imprinted on the instruments and the child can easily play the correct note. He does not have to find where to put his fingers as he would for the violin, recorder, piano, or other instruments.

To be fully meaningful, therefore, and to give the children real experience and understanding of notation, actual performance on instruments is required. The simple activities and games using melody bells and Swiss Melody Bells which are included here, can help the child learn the notation easily and pleasantly so that he can have the joy and satisfaction of making and understanding music.

GROUP GAMES AND CLASS ACTIVITIES

Walk the Notes

Prepare a "floor staff." Draw the five-line staff using a thick marker on a long roll of wrapping paper. Or else, prepare a "floor staff" by putting five strips of colored adhesive tape on the floor. Allow plenty of room for this activity. The staff can be placed between rows of desks or in front of the room. One child starts by standing at the left of the floor staff on the first line. As you play tones on the melody bells, the child walks "up" and "down" the staff according to the pitch of the tones being played.

Pitch Notation Bingo (Note-O)

Prepare cards for Pitch Notation Bingo, each one different and each showing six notes and 𝄞. 𝄞 is "Free," and is covered with a disc cut out of black construction paper. As the teacher calls out the names of the notes, the children cover those they have with discs. The first one to cover all the notes wins. (For mainstreamed hard-of-hearing children, in addition to calling out the names of the notes, write the name on the board or hold up a card showing the letter name.)

SAMPLE CHART

Note Hop Scotch

Prepare the floor for Hop Scotch. Draw the outline with chalk on the floor or use marker on a sheet of heavy vinyl. The children take turns being "It." "It" throws the beanbag onto the game area and then must name the note (or the music symbol) on which the beanbag lands.

Spin the Arrow

Using a large box cover or a sheet of oaktag, black construction paper for the arrows, and a round-headed paper fastener, prepare a "Spin the Arrow" game with drawings of notes. The children take turns spinning the arrow and naming the note (or groups of notes) to which the arrow points.

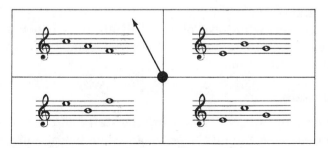

Create Aleatory Melody, or "Mixed-Up Tunes"

Aleatory composition is music created by chance. The composer does not know ahead of time how it will sound. All children, regardless of handicap, can participate in this game. Because melodies are created by chance, no special musical or mental ability is needed.

Have a box of notes drawn on construction paper. There should be enough for each child playing so there may have to be duplicates of some notes. The children come to the front of the room, one row at a time. They each take a note from the box and then stand alongside each other. Whatever notes they hold become the "mixed-up tune" which is played on melody bells by a pupil or the teacher.

Create "Mixed-Up Tunes" (Variation)

Prepare cards, on each of which different notes are drawn. Repeat some of the notes. Have a child come to the front of the room, mix up the cards and arrange them, by chance, in any order at all. Play the resulting aleatory melody on the melody bells.

Create Tunes with Pupils as Notes

This is similar to the preceding games. The pupils are given cards to hold, each one of which has a different note. Repeat some notes if necessary. Have a child act as composer and arrange the children in a row. The children show the cards they hold and the melody is played. If the composer wants to, he rearranges any of the children to improve the song.

Find Your Twin Note

There are two teams. Every child gets a drawing of a note. There are two drawings of each note for each team. At the signal, each one of the children has to find and stand next to the child on his own team who is holding the same note picture. The first team to have all pairs matched wins.

The children who have physical disabilities can participate in this game. They can remain in their seats and their partners can come and sit with them.

Jigsaw Puzzle

Prepare a jigsaw puzzle showing the staff and the notes placed in random order. This can either be mounted on board and used by any of the children during a "free choice" period, or it can be duplicated on paper and distributed to all the children to use at the same time. Cut the puzzle into pieces similar to those in the example, so that the note on the staff and the name of that note would not appear on the same piece of the puzzle. (See the illustration.)

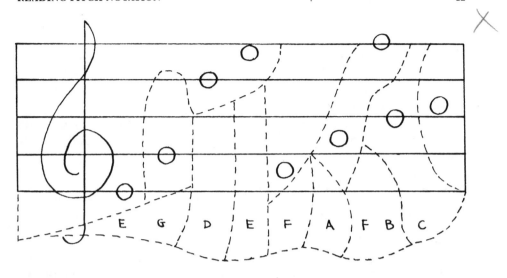

Find Your Name: Find Your Note

This is similar to the game "Find Your Twin Note." There are two teams. Each child on half of each team is given a drawing of a note. The others on the team each receive the name of a note. At the signal, they have to find their partners—the name or note which belongs to the card they hold.

Which Tune Did You Hear?

Three simple melodic groups are written on the chalkboard. Play one of them; then, point to each tone group. Have the children raise their hands to indicate which one they heard. (Start with melodies having obvious differences.)

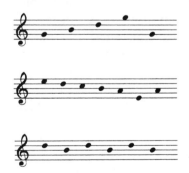

Spelling Bee with Pitch Notation

The class is divided into teams. Use flash cards to show notes. Each correctly identified note earns a point. The first team to earn ten points wins.

Flash Cards

The staff is written with chalk on the board. Show flash cards, each of which has a letter from A to G. The child whose turn it is comes to the front of the room and draws the note on the correct line or space on the staff.

The very slow learner who may find the notation very difficult can participate in the game by being the one to select and hold up the flash cards.

Pin the Note on the Wall Staff

Prepare a wall staff. Draw lines and spaces and a G clef () on a large sheet of plastic or vinyl. The children are given "notes" (circles cut out from black construction paper). Names of notes are called out and the children take turns, each one pinning his or her note on the correct line or space. (A felt board and felt notes can be used for the wall staff.)

Pin the Note on the Wall Staff (Variation)

In this game, several children can be blindfolded and they try to pin their notes on the designated place. The one coming closest wins. (Because this game involves luck, the mentally retarded child can play with equal chance for success.)

Team Races Using the Wall Staff

Prepare a wall staff on a large sheet of heavy colored plastic. Draw the lines and spaces of the staff with marker, or indicate them with lines made with colored tape. The treble clef should be in place.

The class is divided into two teams, each child holding a note—a circle cut out from black construction paper. The teams stand in lines and the teacher calls out the name of a note (e.g., "a," "f on a line," "f inside a space"). The children on each team who are first in line run to the staff and tape or pin their notes in place. The first one to finish wins a point for the team. These two children sit and then the others play in turn.

Floor Staff Tag

Two children play at a time. One child is given a card with the name of a note. At the signal, he has to run "Home"—to the correct position on the floor staff as indicated by the card. If he gets to the correct spot without being tagged by the other child, who is "It," he is "safe." (The mentally retarded can easily participate in this game. Those having too much difficulty remembering notation can be "It.")

Which Note Is This?

Write a note on the staff drawn on the chalkboard. The children study the note, deciding what it is, and then cover their eyes, placing their heads down on their desks. Call out different names for the note, including impossible answers. The children raise their hands, without peeking, when they hear the correct answer.

On chalkboard

Call out "g! b! a! q! s! (expect laughter here) c!"

(This is a good, quick informal evaluation of pupils' knowledge of pitch notation.)

Who's on First (Line)?

Use the floor staff. Have five children stand on the different lines of the floor staff (not in consecutive order). Five other children are each given a card with the name of a line (E,G,B,D, and F). At the given signal, each child runs to the child standing on the line represented by the card he holds, gives that child the card, and then returns to his place. The same thing can be done with just space notes and then with all notes, lines and spaces.

(The mentally retarded child can readily participate by being one of those standing in place on the staff.)

Play What You See

Notes are written on the chalkboard in any order. Then, children come to the board and write the correct names. The Swiss Melody Bells are distributed, one for each note written on the board. The children holding the bells stand in front of their notes and play what is written.

Then the names are erased and the bells are distributed to other children who, taking the places of the first group, play the written notes. (See the illustration.)

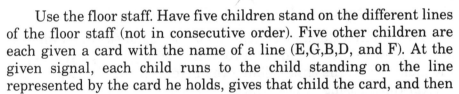

Find the Note on the Hand Staff

Use the hand as the staff, and give each finger a name. The thumb is e, the pointer is g, the middle finger is b, etc. The children hold their hands horizontally. As the name of the note is called, the appropriate finger is wriggled for a line note, or the space is pointed to for a space note.

Find the Teacher's Mistake

Place felt notes on a felt board to form simple phrases from well-known melodies. Have one wrong note (see illustration). The children identify the notes and play the melody on the melody bells. They will hear (to their delight) the teacher's "mistake." One child is asked to come to the felt board and try to change the wrong note to the correct one on the felt board.

Name the Note Game (Note, Note, Who's Got the Note?)

The children stand in a circle and pass around a card on which a note is drawn. They do this as a recording of music is played. When the music stops, the child holding the note identifies it. Repeat this several times, using different notes.

Find the Pitch Level

On the chalkboard, draw a picture of a man with lines extending from his body at five levels—knees, hips, waist, shoulders, face. (See the illustration.)

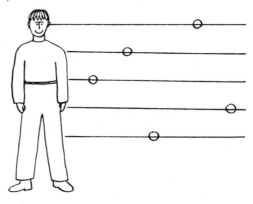

As you point to the different lines, the children place their hands at the same points on their own bodies. Then, as the children continue to touch their own bodies, a child points to the different lines at random and the teacher plays the note (e, g, b, d, or f) which appears at the designated level.

Now, the drawing is erased with just the lines remaining. The game is repeated with only the lines as guides.

Be a Composer

Distribute music paper to the children and have them compose their own melodies—writing notes anywhere on the staff. Then, have them trade papers and play each other's tunes on the melody bells.

Color the Repeated Patterns

Place the notation of a very familiar short song with repeated melodic patterns on the chalkboard or on a chart. Have the children sing the song. Now, ask the children to raise their hands when they hear any part repeated, and have selected children color the notes of the repeated melodic patterns with the same color.

TWINKLE, TWINKLE, LITTLE STAR

Board Game (Become a Musician!)

This game can be played by several children. Use notes cut out of black construction paper as markers. The children spin an arrow on a dial which indicates how many boxes to move forward. The rules would be the same as for any similar board game.

Find the Missing Note

On the chalkboard or on a chart, write a brief, familiar melody leaving out the last note. (A music felt board with staff can be used. This can be easily prepared by covering a large piece of stiff cardboard with felt. Then, take pieces of cord of a contrasting color and tie these around the board to form the staff. This can be a permanent staff, always ready for various music games and activities.)

Play the melody using the melody bells, but omit the last note. One child then reads and plays the tune, trying to find the last note. When he discovers what it should be, he writes the note in the correct place (or places it on the felt board). This activity can be varied by leaving out other tones.

Can You Play the Tune?

Write a number of notes in random order on a chart or chalk-board. One of the children is the conductor, pointing to any of the notes. A second child plays the indicated note on the Swiss Melody Bells. If he makes a mistake, the child who can correct it takes his place at the bells and another child becomes the conductor.

Singing from a Two-Line Staff

This should be done only following repeated experience and practice with the Kodaly hand signals (discussed in Chapter 1). The children should be able to sing from hand signals indicating "sol-mi" and "mi-re-do."

Tell the class, "Instead of showing you what to sing by signaling with my hands, I am going to write signs on the board."

On a two-line staff, write:

Children practice singing the tones as you point to them. Then, you write these tones at random and the children sing what they see:

Singing Pitch from a Three-Line Staff

The same activity as the above can be done using the syllables "do-re-mi." The teacher draws a three-line staff and labels it:

These notes are, after some practice, written at random and the children sing them.

Singing from a Three-Line Staff (Variation)

The two tone groups, "so-mi" and "do-re-mi" (or "mi-re-do") can now be combined:

PAPER AND PENCIL GAMES AND ACTIVITIES

Write Notes Up and Down the Steps

Provide work sheets with drawings of steps going up and down. Play tones on the melody bells and have the children write circles on the appropriate steps to show the pitch going up or down.

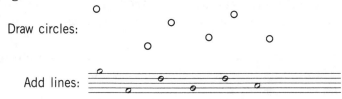

Write Circles, Add Lines

As you play tones on the melody bells, have the children draw circles on a sheet of paper to indicate whether the sound is getting higher or lower. Then, using a ruler, have them draw five lines on the page.

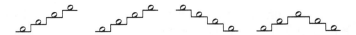

(Note: Accuracy is not essential here. The purpose is to have the children see that the notes on the lines and inside the spaces *show* the sound going up and down.)

Which Way Are the Notes Going?

Provide work sheets on which "people" notes are drawn "walking" uphill, downhill or "standing still." The children number their pages from 1-5. Play a series of tones. If the notes go "uphill," the children write letter "A"; "B" if they go "downhill"; "C" if they repeat. Five examples are played.

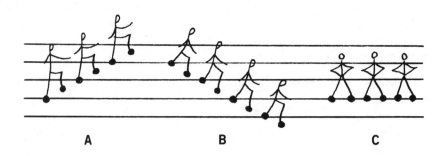

Find the Repeated Notes

Distribute work sheets showing the staff with a series of notes. The children draw a slur (curved line) over any two or more adjacent notes which repeat.

Find the Different Notes

Distribute work sheets with a series of paired melodic fragments. The children find the notes in each pair which are different from each other.

Write Up and Down Tunes

Distribute work sheets showing the music staff, or music manuscript paper. Have the children draw (1) repeated notes (2) notes going up (3) notes going down. (The G clef need not be included. The purpose of this activity is to relate the sound of pitch going up and down with the appearance of notes going up and down the staff.) Have individual children play what they have written on the melody bells.

Repeat, this time having the children write, in any order, notes going up, down, or repeating. Have them play what they have written.

Follow the Tune

Provide work sheets showing the scores of brief, simple, familiar melodies. As you sing the tunes or play them on the melody bells, the children draw contour lines to show the shape of the melody as it goes up and down in pitch.

MERRILY WE ROLL ALONG

Find the Line Notes

Distribute work sheets with notes on the lines and spaces. Have the children circle the notes on the lines.

Find the Space Notes

Distribute work sheets with notes on the lines and the spaces. Have the children color the notes inside the spaces with any colors they choose.

Find the Skipping and Walking Note People

Draw "note people" walking up and down the staff and skipping up and down. Point to different examples and have the children take turns playing what they see on the melody bells. (See the illustration.)

(Accuracy in playing specific notes is not essential. This activity can be done before the children know the names of the lines and spaces. The purpose is to recognize the relationship between the sound and the appearance of notes moving step-by-step or skipping.)

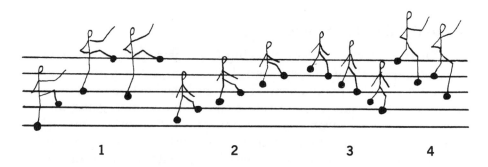

      1   2   3   4

Find the Skipping and Walking Notes

Repeat the above activity, this time writing the notes.

Are the Notes Walking or Skipping?

Place on the chalkboard or a chart, pictures of "skipping" and "walking" notes, going up and down. Play an example of one of them on the melody bells. Have one child come to the front of the room and point to the one he hears. If he is correct, he becomes "It" and has a turn playing an example.

Which Notes Walk? Which Notes Skip?

The children are given work sheets showing examples of "note people" walking and skipping up and down the staff. They write in the allotted space the words "skip" or "walk," depending on the example. (See the illustration.)

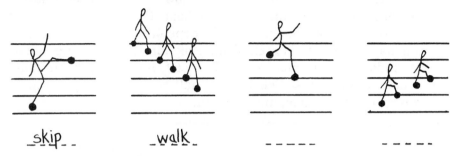

skip _   _walk_   _ _ _ _ _   _ _ _ _ _

Find the Skips

The children are given work sheets showing notes going up and down the staff. They mark those notes which are "skipping."

Write Walking and Skipping Notes

The children are given music manuscript paper and write notes walking or skipping up or down, according to instructions.

Find the Hidden Music Words (Puzzle)

The children look for the following words that are hidden in the square: f-a-c-e (the names of the space notes), staff, treble, note, clef, line, space. They can be found in the boxes, spelled horizontally or vertically.

S	T	A	F	F	S
N	R	L	A	N	P
O	E	I	C	O	A
T	B	N	E	T	C
C	L	E	F	E	E
R	E	T	N	O	B

Find the Hidden Music Signs

Show the class the illustration below. The picture contains rhythm, pitch notation, and other symbols. It can be modified to include or omit various music symbols, depending on which ones the children have learned. The children look for the following music symbols hidden in the picture: staff, G clef, half note, whole note, eighth note, quarter rest, whole rest, half rest, eighth rest, repeat sign, sharp, common time, and fermata.

FIND THE MUSIC SIGNS

Can you find these music signs? They are all hiding in the picture.

Staff	Three quarter notes
G clef	Four eighth notes
Two whole note rests	Two half notes
Two half note rests	Eighth note rest
Sharp	Fermata
Repeat sign	Music staff
Common time	Three quarter note rests
Four whole notes	

Make a Hand Staff

Have the child make a tracing of his hand on a large sheet of construction paper. Then, extend lines from the five fingers to make a "Hand Staff." (See the illustration.) This emphasizes the fact that the staff has five lines and four spaces in between them. Later, after the G clef has been learned, the names of the notes can be written on the lines and inside the spaces of the Hand Staff.

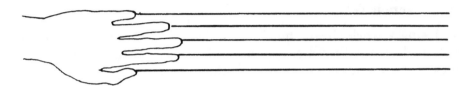

Follow the Dots to Make a G Clef

Help the children learn to write the G (treble) clef by using a dot-to-dot diagram.

Write the G Clef

Provide a work sheet with the G clef written in stages. Have the children copy each stage.

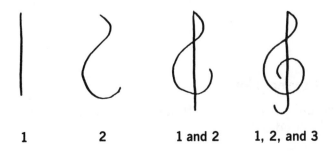

| 1 | 2 | 1 and 2 | 1, 2, and 3 |

Make G Clefs from Pipe Cleaners

Each child is given a pipe cleaner and bends it into the shape of a G, or treble, clef 𝄞. These can be pasted onto colored construction paper on which the children have drawn the staff. Notes can then be cut out from black construction paper and pasted on the staff. The pipe cleaner clefs can also be attached with safety pins to the children's collars or shirts.

Which Note is G?

Using a work sheet, the children draw a G clef on the staff. A circle is drawn with red crayon around the second line. A row of G notes is then written on the second line.

Find the Gs

Distribute work sheets showing notes written at random on the staff with the G clef. Have the children color the circle around the second line. Then, have them find all the G notes on the staff and color them in. (Free use of color is suggested.)

Find the Teacher's Mistake

Distribute work sheets on which you write and label the notes, making several deliberate errors. The children are to find the mistakes and correct them.

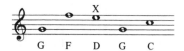

Color the Correct Note

Distribute work sheets with a series of notes. The children color in the designated note.

Color in the Cs

Color in *ALL* the Es

Add the Stems

The children are given work sheets showing notes without stems placed in random order. They are to add the stems in the correct direction. (All notes above the third line B should have stems going down. Notes below B have stems going up. B can be written with the stem going up or down.)

Name the Note

Give the children work sheets showing the staff, the G clef, and notes written in random order. The children identify and write the names of the notes.

Write the Named Note

This is more difficult than the previous activities and should be introduced when the children can easily identify the written notes.

Distribute work sheets with names of notes. Have the children write the notes in the correct positions.

Write Music Words

Many words can be written with the letters A, B, C, D, E, F, and G.

1. Have the children write the names of the notes and then read the resulting words.

   B E A D   F A C E   D E A D

2. Give them the words; have the children write the notes.

   C A B B A G E   B E D   F A D E

3. The children figure out words using the letters and then write the notes that spell those words.

Match the Note

Distribute work sheets showing two columns. In one column, the letters A, B, C, D, E, F, G are listed. In the second column, the notes on the lines and spaces of the staff are listed in random order. The children draw lines connecting the name of the note to the correct symbol.

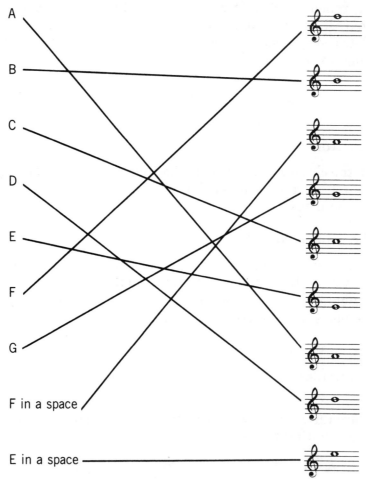

A
B
C
D
E
F
G
F in a space
E in a space

A Music Story

Write a music story using as many words made up of the letters from A to G as you possibly can. Have the children write the names of the notes to complete the story. (Bright, creative children will be able to make up their own music stories.)

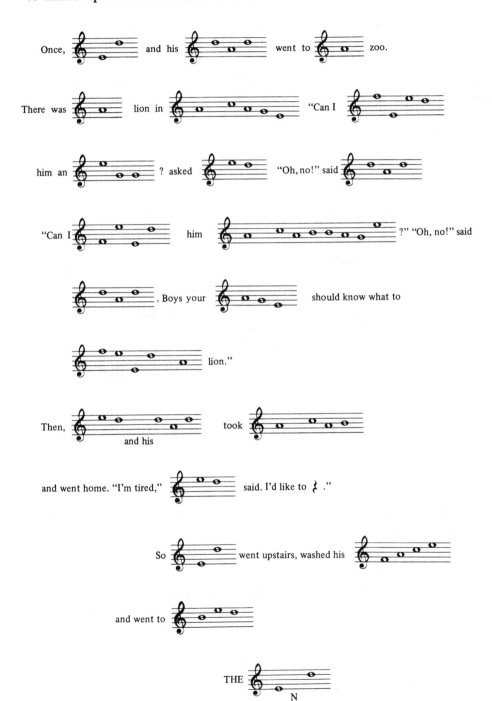

Once, [music] and his [music] went to [music] zoo.

There was [music] lion in [music] "Can I

him an [music] ? asked [music] "Oh, no!" said [music]

"Can I [music] him [music] ?" "Oh, no!" said

[music] . Boys your [music] should know what to

[music] lion."

Then, [music] and his [music] took [music]

and went home. "I'm tired," [music] said. I'd like to ♪ ."

So [music] went upstairs, washed his [music]

and went to [music]

THE [music]
N

MUSIC NOTATION AND MAINSTREAMING

There are children in the mainstreamed class who may have difficulty recognizing, learning, or remembering the names of the notes on the staff. There is no reason, however, that they cannot participate in reading and performing music. They can achieve the same feeling of accomplishment as the other children—the same emotional joy and aesthetic appreciation. Also, they can be part of the group while they experience making music with others. The child's self image, coordination, and social relationships can all be enhanced.

One of the ways this can be accomplished is through the use of color coding, as in the following activities.

Color Coding

Draw blocks of color to represent the colored Swiss Melody Bells; each note will be represented by its own color. (See the illustration.) This can be done using a chart or by preparing special scores for the children who need them. The children stand in a row, each one holding a different bell. Then, reading left to right, they play the bells in turn, as indicated by the colored blocks.

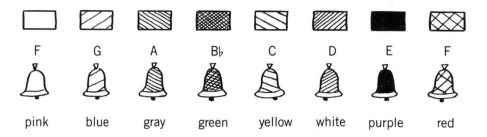

This activity also emphasizes that reading proceeds from left to right and helps to review matching and recognition of colors.

Play the Melody from the Notes

Charts of simple melodies are prepared, each note having its own color—the same color as that of the Swiss Melody Bell which plays that tone. Children play the bell having the same color as the note.

gray blue pink   gray blue pink   pink   pink   blue   blue   gray blue pink
                                            pink pink blue blue

The same sort of color coding can be used in all the "playing from note" games. Another way to bring the child with learning difficulties into the activities is to have him be the one to hold the cards, distribute cards, be the conductor who points to the notes or to the other children who will play the notes, or be the composer who arranges the notes in random order.

3

Developing the Sense of Rhythm

BODY MOVEMENT

In order for a child to intellectually understand the rhythms of music, he must first be able to feel and experience them. The best way to develop this feeling is through the use of body movement.

The child's world is filled with rhythmic sounds and movements and our bodies have their own rhythmic patterns. The purpose of the following games and activities is to make the child aware of this world of rhythm so that he can develop his sensitivity to sound and his ability to coordinate his body in a controlled, relaxed rhythmic response.

If you have a piano available and the ability to improvise, this would provide, on occasion, an excellent accompaniment for the following movement activities. Not only can a beat be established in this way, but the different harmonies, melodic patterns, and dynamics can supply backgrounds with varied moods. For those who cannot play an instrument, however, the drum is very suitable and satisfactory. With it, you can set the beat and lead all the activities. Because it is simple to use and the best percussion instrument for the purpose, its use is suggested throughout this chapter.

Guess the Work Activity

Pantomime hammering and ask, "What am I doing?" When the children guess correctly, ask them to think of some work they can do (e.g.: sawing wood, using a jackhammer, chopping trees, typing a letter, carrying a load). Have volunteers act out the work activity while the rest of the class tries to guess what "It" is doing. When the

61

correct answer is given, have the whole class do the activity and as they do, beat a drum in time to their movements. Repeat the game several times, calling on different children. The sound of the drum and the feel of the movement will vary in tempo and rhythmic pattern for the different activities.

Guess the Play Activity

Pantomime a sport or play activity (e.g.: bouncing a ball, rocking a doll, swimming, dribbling a basketball and shooting for the basket, kicking a football, jumping rope). After the children guess the activity, call on volunteers to act out different play or sport activities. When the class guesses the activity, have them do the movements to the beat of the drum.

Follow the Drum

Tell the children that the drum is going to "talk" to them. When the drum beat is fast, they are to clap fast. When the beat is slow, they are to clap slowly. If the drum stops, they stop. Play a steady beat on the drum and have the children clap. Vary the tempo; play very slowly, at a moderate rate of speed, or quickly. Sometimes start or stop suddenly to add the element of surprise.

Clap the Name

Ask a child to say his name. Then repeatedly clap the rhythmic pattern of the name. Have the children join you. Repeat the activity using a number of children's names.

Stamp the Name

After a child gives his or her name, have the children stand and stamp their feet a number of times to the rhythm of the name. (The same activity can be done with other movements—tapping the desk, snapping fingers, etc. In this way, children with physical disabilities can easily participate.)

Move the Windmill

Have the children pretend to be windmills as they "move" their hands in a revolving motion. As you beat the drum in various tempos, they move their hands faster or slower in response.

Have a Slow-Motion Race

It is usually easier for young children to move at a moderate or quick tempo than at a slow rate of speed. This activity can help to develop more body control. Tell the children that they will have a "Slow-Motion Race." Select three or four children at a time. They are to move across the room as slowly as they can. The movements must be flowing and continuous as in a slow-motion movie and the last one to reach the other side of the room wins the race.

Getting Fast and Getting Slow

In these activities, the children pretend to be different things which can get fast (*accelerando*) or get slow (*ritardando*).

Horses

Vary the drum beat as the children play that they are horses. Start at a walk, gradually increase the tempo to a trotting, a cantering, and finally, a galloping rhythm. Gradually play more slowly as the children change their movements from a gallop to a canter, then a trot, a walk, and finally stand still.

Trains

The children form short lines, each one holding the elbows of the child in front of him. Beat the drum slowly. They start shuffling slowly. As the tempo of the drum beats increases, the children move faster. Then they gradually slow down with the slower tempo of the drum, until they stop.

Those children who cannot do the movement activity because of physical disabilities can accompany the action by playing maracas, sandpaper blocks, or whistles in time to the drum. This will provide excellent sound effects in imitation of the sound of a train.

Dance to Music Using Scarves

Distribute several colorful scarves and have the children move (dance) to the music of various recordings, waving the scarves in any way they want to.

Play "Freeze"

Have a group of children dance to recordings. Vary the tempo, type, and mood of the music. When the record is stopped, they are to "freeze" and remain in the position in which they are. Repeat this a number of times to give them the opportunity to express various types of music. (Many boys are shy or self-conscious about dancing and this activity can help in such cases. Just don't use the word "dance." Tell the class that they will play a game and that they are to move to the music. They will probably begin to participate and, after a while, begin to respond to the music with their body movements.) Children with physical disabilities can move their arms, heads, or legs as they remain at their desks and "freeze" in position as the music stops.

Be the Conductor

Play a suitable recording and have the children make believe that they are conductors. Try to select compositions with varying moods and tempos. Among other possible pieces, you could play the Hungarian Dance No. 5 by Brahms, "The Anvil Chorus" by Verdi, or selections from *Carmen Suite* by Bizet. These works contain changes in mood and tempo and are therefore especially suitable for the activity. These works can be found on the recording *Conduct Your Own Orchestra,* Golden Record GLP 47.

Act Out a Story

Have the children listen to a record and create a story they feel is suitable to express the music. Then, have them act out the story in pantomime as the music is played.

Helping the Arrhythmic Child

Some children cannot keep in time to music, even after many activities and experiences such as the preceding ones. When the other children clap, march, or stamp to music, the arrhythmic children seem to be literally moving to another drummer. Avoid calling attention to this condition. Instead, try the following activities which can be helpful to them and are also fine for developing the sense of rhythm in all children.

Swing Your Arms with a Partner

Children take their partners' hands and swing their arms in time to the drumbeat. An arrhythmic child, paired with a child who has a strong sense of rhythm, will find himself moved along by the partner and will begin to get the feel of moving to music.

Play Push and Pull

Children take their partner's hands and, as the drum beats, they move their arms alternately in a "push-pull" movement, extending first one arm and then the other.

Ring the Bells

The children take their partners' hands and, as the drum beats slowly, they pretend to be ringing huge bells, swaying to the rhythm of the drum.

Play "See-Saw"

The children take their partners' hands and then play "see-saw" to the beat of the drum or to the chant:

> See-saw,
> Margery Daw,
> Johnny shall have a new master.
> He shall get but a penny a day,
> Because he can't work any faster.

As one child bends his knees to go down, the other one stands. Then they switch positions. (See the illustration.)

SEE   —   SAW

Swing in a Circle

Have the children form a circle and take each others' hands. Place the arrhythmic child between two children who move well to music. As you play a drum, have them swing their arms forward and back to the rhythm. Vary the tempo, but do not play too quickly.

March Shoulder to Shoulder

Have a parade with the children marching three abreast, shoulders touching. Place the arrhythmic child between two children who have strong rhythmic responses so that he will be carried along by the impetus.

Move the Way the Drum Tells You To

Have the children listen to the drum and decide whether you are playing a walking, a running, a skipping, a galloping, a jumping-rope, or a digging-a-ditch rhythm. They then move to the rhythm being played.

After they can recognize them, have them move to the rhythms as you change from one to the other.

Learn to Conduct:

Teach the children the basic conducting beats for a march (⅔) and for a waltz (¾). Have them conduct waltzes and marches using the patterns shown in the illustration.

Stamp the Meter

As the children listen to a slow waltz, have them stamp their feet (or clap their hands) on the strong beat and say "One!" on the strong beat:

1 2 3, 1 2 3, 1 2 3, 1, 2, 3

Do the same thing for the music in 2's and 4's:

1, 2, 1, 2, 1, 2, 1, 2
or
1, 2, 3, 4, 1, 2, 3, 4, 1, 2, 3, 4

Bounce the Ball to the Meter

Using a large medicine ball, let the children take turns bouncing the ball on the strong beat of the music. Use music with very definite rhythms.

Play Ball to the Meter

Let two children play catch with a large medicine ball, throwing the ball to each other on the strong beats of the selected music. (You can also do this with one child.)

Pass the Ball

Have the children stand in a circle. Play music with a clear, strongly accentuated rhythm. Have them move a large medicine ball around the circle, passing it to the next child on the strong beat of the music.

Exercise to Music

Play a recording of music with a very strong beat and have the children do setting-up exercises to it.

Play Twos, Threes, or Fours

Divide the class into three groups—the "two's," the "three's" and the "four's." In random order, play music having the different meters—$\frac{2}{4}$, $\frac{3}{4}$, and $\frac{4}{4}$. Children belonging to the appropriate group move in any way they choose to their own music when it is played. (Children with physical disabilities can easily participate by waving their arms, tapping their desks, nodding their heads, or tapping their feet, etc.)

Play Rhythm Charades

Each pupil picks (from a basket) a slip of paper on which is written a rhythm activity (e.g.: jump rope, chop wood, move like a rabbit, imitate raindrops, move your arms like a clock, play tennis, row a boat, do the backstroke, be a piston). The child has to act out the movement until the rest of the class guesses what the action signifies.

Echo the Rhythm

Play a brief rhythmic pattern on the drum and have the children echo the sound by clapping their hands, stamping their feet, or tapping their desks. Gradually increase the length and difficulty of the rhythmic pattern to be echoed.

Play Rhythm Follow the Leader

Play a brief rhythm on the drum and have the children clap back the echo. Repeat the rhythm, but this time, as the children clap the rhythm, they are to listen to you play a second simple rhythmic pattern and clap that one. Repeat the whole activity, adding a third pattern as the children clap the second one. See how many patterns they can follow. This activity is not a simple one and takes intense concentration and control. At first, you may find that the children can only clap back two patterns. Little by little, as their memory for rhythms and their ability to concentrate improves, they will be able

Teacher plays:

Children clap back:

Two patterns:
Teacher:

Children:

Three patterns:
Teacher:

Children:

to clap back additional patterns. The resulting sound is called imitation in music and is similar in effect to a round.

Make a Sound with Your Body

Have the children create a rhythmic pattern and then have them figure out different ways they can use different parts of their bodies to make the pattern. Each resulting sound will be different. Children can clap, tap their fingers on their desks, stamp their feet, snap their fingers, make clicking sounds with their tongues, tap their wrists, rub their feet against the floor, hit the floor with their heels, tap their toes on the floor, slap their thighs, make vocal sounds, clap with cupped palms, hit the desk with their fists, or think of other activities.

Play Rhythm "Simple Simon"

Play a variation of "Simple Simon." Tell the children to do what you do if you say "Simple Simon says do this." Perform repeated rhythmic movements as the children imitate you. If you do not say, "Simple Simon says...," they are to remain still. Let different children be "Simon."

Step the Song

Instead of clapping the rhythm of a song, as a familiar tune is sung by the class, have some of the children step on every note of the melody.

Play Rhythm Hot or Cold

One child is chosen to be "It" and goes out of the room. An object is hidden. When "It" returns, she makes up a rhythmic pattern and as the rest of the class begins to clap the rhythm, "It" tries to find the object. The closer "It" gets to the object, the faster the pattern is clapped. The farther away from the object, the slower the pattern is clapped.

Do Other Movements with Your Body

Many other movements can be suggested by music in addition to the ones described in the preceding activities. The children can hop, skip, shake their shoulders, crawl, wiggle, rock, twirl, shake their heads, or move their bodies to create any movement they can think of as music in various tempos, rhythmic patterns, and moods is played.

RHYTHM BAND INSTRUMENTS

When distributing rhythm band instruments, remember that a pleasing sound is important. If too many children have instruments, they tend to play so enthusiastically that the music or song to which they are playing, or the rhythmic pattern they are to follow, is drowned out. Therefore, in order to avoid having them play faster and faster and louder and louder, it is a good idea to limit the number of instruments being used at any one time to perhaps seven to ten. Don't worry about not giving all the children instruments at the same time. Children are used to—or should be used to—taking turns. The next time—we hope these activities will be repeated many times—a different group of children can be given the instruments.

Play Rhythm Band Echoes

Distribute instruments. Play a rhythm on the drum. Have the children take turns echoing the rhythmic pattern on their own instruments.

Follow the Leader

As in the "clap-back" game, beat a rhythmic pattern and have the children imitate it. Then, the next time, as they imitate your pattern, they hear a second pattern which they will imitate. Continue the game, having them follow your lead as long as they can.

Ask a Rhythm Question; Give a Rhythm Answer

Distribute instruments. "Ask a question" by playing a rhythmic pattern on the drum. As you finish, immediately point to one of the children. This child "answers" your "question" by replying on a different instrument with a different rhythmic pattern. He is not supposed to repeat what you have played, but rather, to create his own rhythm.

Continue the Story

Distribute instruments to about ten children and have them stand in a row in front of the room. Play a rhythmic pattern. When you have finished, point to the first child in the row who will continue the "story" by playing any rhythmic pattern suggested by what you played. As he or she finishes, the next child in the row plays and then the next, and so on. Encourage the children to make up their own rhythms.

Play Your Name

Give each child a chance to come to the front of the room, state his or her name, and then play several times the rhythmic pattern of the name on any instrument of his or her choice. A great number of attractive rhythmic patterns played on various instruments will result in a variety of interesting sounds.

Play All the Names Together

Let each child who has played his or her name on an instrument retain the instrument. Establish a steady beat and then, at a signal from you, have them all play together, each one playing his or her own rhythm. An interesting and exciting combination of tone qualities and rhythms should result. Possible rhythmic combinations could include some like the following:

Have a Rhythm Roll Call

Tell the children that instead of calling out their names, you will take the roll call by playing the names on the drum. Go down your list of pupils and play the rhythmic patterns indicated by the names. The children whose names fit any of the patterns stand.

Have a Group Improvisation

This can be done with about fifteen children. Distribute varied instruments and start to beat a steady beat on the drum. Point to one pupil who will begin to play any rhythmic pattern that he or she chooses to the beat you have established. Point to others, one at a time, gradually adding more and more instruments until all are creating their own patterns to the basic beat. Suggest that the children vary their patterns if they want to and you, too, can have fun varying your own rhythmic patterns.

Have a "Jam" Session

As above, start a group improvisation. When everyone is playing, point to one musician who will take the solo—playing whatever he or she pleases while the rest of the group play their instruments very softly as an accompaniment. As that pupil finishes, all play together again until the next soloist is picked.

Conduct the Band

Select a child to be the conductor and the chief composer or organizer of the music. He or she sets the beat, calls on different players to start or to stop playing, and indicates who the soloists should be and when the playing should be louder or softer.

Guess the Song

Beat out the rhythm of the words of a song with which the children are very familiar, and have them guess the name of the song. If they cannot recognize the song, give them a hint (e.g., for "America" — "This is a patriotic song"; for Brahms' "Lullabye" — "This song can make you sleepy"). Add one hint at a time until the correct song is named. Have the children take turns being the one to play a song rhythm for the others to guess.

Play the Given Tempo

Teach the musical terms for "very slow" (*largo*), "moderate rate of speed" (*moderato*), and "fast," (*allegro*). Distribute rhythm instruments and divide the children into three groups—Largo, Moderato, and Allegro. Put the three indications on the chalkboard and then clap or play a brief rhythmic pattern on the drum. Have the children echo the rhythm on their instruments. Then, as you point, in turn, to the different terms, the children in the specified group play the given pattern in the tempo indicated. Help them stay together by conducting the rhythmic beat desired. The children can take turns playing the instruments and pointing to the different tempo indications.

Change the Tempo

Teach the terms *accelerando* (gradually get faster) and *ritardando* (gradually get slower). Have a child create a rhythmic pattern and play it on any rhythm instrument of his or her choice. Write the words *accelerando* and *ritardando* on the chalkboard and pick a second child to be the conductor. As the conductor points to the terms, the child playing the rhythmic pattern accordingly plays it getting faster or slower.

Move Like an Instrument

Let the children discuss how they would move to express the sound of different rhythm instruments. Rhythm sticks could suggest short, sharp, stiff movements; triangles could suggest gentle, somewhat sustained ones. Crashing cymbals could be shown by a leap or any sudden, large movement followed by a slow one gradually becoming smaller as the sound of the cymbals fades. Shaking tambourines might be expressed by a trembling.

After the movement is decided, have one group play short, rhythmic patterns on any of the instruments while other children move to the rhythms to express the instrument being played.

MISCELLANEOUS ACTIVITIES

Find Rhythm in the Environment

Have the children think of and make a list of things in the environment that have regular, even rhythmic patterns (e.g.: the patter of rain, the dripping of a water faucet, clocks ticking, trains chugging, waves breaking, children running, motors turning).

Make a Rhythm Bulletin Board

Have the children bring in or draw pictures of things in the environment that have steady, even rhythmic patterns, and use these illustrations to make a "Rhythm Bulletin Board."

Find Your Own Body Rhythm

Show the children how to take a pulse. As they find their own, have them wave their hands in time to the pulsations they feel. Call on different children to demonstrate and time some of the beats and compare them.

Let the children see that, although individuals differ in their basic body rhythms, the pulse beat reflects the same essential function for all of them.

Find Examples of Tempo

Have the children make two lists—one of things that move quickly (e.g., airplanes, automobiles, birds, race horses, rabbits, people running), and one of things that move slowly (turtles, oxcarts, snails, babies toddling). Label the lists *Allegro* and *Largo*.

Make a Tempo Chart

Using the list they have developed, have the children make a "Tempo Chart." They can bring in or draw pictures and paste them onto a chart with columns labeled *Allegro* and *Largo*.

Name the Tempo

Teach additional tempo indications: *andante*–slowly; *presto*–very quickly; *moderato*–at a moderate rate of speed. Have the children write next to each item on a list of moving objects the name of the tempo of its movement.

airplane	*presto*
rockets	*presto*
man running	*allegro*
turtle	*largo*
people walking	*moderato*

Arrange the Tempos in Order

Distribute worksheets on which are listed a number of moving objects. Have two columns—one labeled *accelerando* (gradually get faster) and the other labeled *ritardando* (gradually get slower). Have the children arrange the items in the correct order to illustrate the concepts *accelerando* and *ritardando*.

Create Word Chants

The use of word chants to develop the sense of rhythm and the ability to read rhythm notation is one of the major features of the Orff Method. This approach to teaching music was developed and systematized by the outstanding contemporary composer, Carl Orff.

Using any suitable subject as a theme, have the children create word chants. This is done by having them make up and repeat again and again, several short sentences or groups of words, so that rhythmic patterns are formed. Once they have decided on the word groups, the children are divided into sections, each of which chants one of the phrases. They can start one after the other, or all or several of the word groups can be chanted together. Changing the combinations of word groups to be chanted at the same time will result in a varied and interesting counterpoint.

Given the topic "Summer Holidays," for example, something like the following might be developed:

Diagram the Rhythmic Pattern

Play a brief rhythmic pattern and have the children draw short and long dashes to illustrate what they have heard:

Chant a Poem

Have the class sing a familiar song and then repeat it using a neutral syllable such as "ta," "da," or "la," instead of words. Now have them chant only the rhythmic patterns of the words of the song using the neutral syllable and omitting both the melody and the words.

Sing with Movement

There are many songs that are intended to be sung with gestures and many others to which gestures can be added. These movements, done in time to music, add more fun to the singing and help to develop the sense of rhythm. Some of the favorites call on the children to decide their own motions or to supply their own words.

ROW YOUR BOAT

TRADITIONAL ROUND

Row, row, row your boat, gen - tly down the stream,___

Mer - ri - ly, mer - ri - ly, mer - ri - ly, mer - ri - ly, Life is but a dream.___

Words	Motions
Row ... your boat	Rowing motion
Gently down the stream	Waving arms gently in
	undulating movement
Merrily....	Clapping hands
Life is but a dream	Eyes closed, resting cheek on
	two hands

The gestures can be done as the song is sung as a round. In this way, as all the groups sing together, each will be moving in a different way.

EXERCISE SONG; TO THE TUNE OF "YANKEE DOODLE"

TRADITIONAL

First you touch your head and then, then you touch your nose; your

cheeks, your lips, and then your hips, and then you touch your toes - o!

A game can be played with this exercise song. Each time the song is repeated, keep all the movements but leave out one more name of a part of the body to be touched. Finally, as the game ends, the children are doing all the motions but omitting the words "head," "nose," "cheeks," "lips," "hips," and "toes."

This type of activity is valuable for a number of reasons. The children are coordinating body movements with song; they are required to *think* and remember the words, melody and rhythm of the song without hearing the sounds; and they are getting the physical benefits of exercise together with the fun of a game.

UNDER THE SPREADING CHESTNUT TREE

TRADITIONAL

Un - der the spread - ing chest - nut tree, There we sat just you and me,

Oh, how hap - py we will be, Un - der the spread - ing chest - nut tree.

Words	Motions
Under the	Point down.
spreading	Hold arms outstretched.
chest	Point to chest.
nut	Tap head.
tree	Stretch arms overhead.
There we sat ...	Bounce a little in seat.
just you	Point to someone else.
and me	Point to self.
Oh, how happy we would be	Clap hands.
Under the spreading....	Repeat motions as at start of song.

Keep the gestures and eliminate one word at a time. As the song is repeated, additional words are dropped and by the time the game is completed, the whole song is thought silently and only the gestures remain.

MY HAT

GERMAN FOLK SONG

Mein Hut, er hat drei Ecke,
Drei Ecke hat mein Hut,
Und ei er hat kein Ecke,
Es sei nicht nur mein Hut.

Words	Motions
My (mein)	Point to self.
hat (Hut)	Tap head.
three (drei)	Hold up three fingers.
corners	Touch one elbow, then the other.
no (kein)	Shake head.
not (nicht)	Shake head.

As in the "Exercise Song" and "Under the Spreading Chestnut Tree," this song can be sung a number of times, each time keeping all the gestures and eliminating additional words each time the song is repeated.

IF YOU'RE HAPPY

AMERICAN SINGING GAME

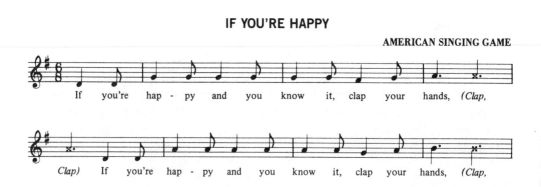

Clap) If you're hap-py and you know it, then your face will sure-ly

show it, If you're hap-py and you know it, clap and hands. *(Clap,   Clap)*

Have the children suggest different words for each verse and suit the actions to the words. Sing this as a cumulative song, each time repeating the words and actions of the previous verses.

Verse 2: Stamp your feet (clap your hands)
Verse 3: Tap your heads (stamp your feet,
  clap your hands)
Verse 4: Hit your desk (tap your head,
  stamp your feet, clap your hands)
Verse 5: Smile a lot (hit your desk, tap your
  heads, stamp your feet, clap your
  hands)

SHE'LL BE COMIN' 'ROUND THE MOUNTAIN

SOUTHERN MOUNTAIN SONG

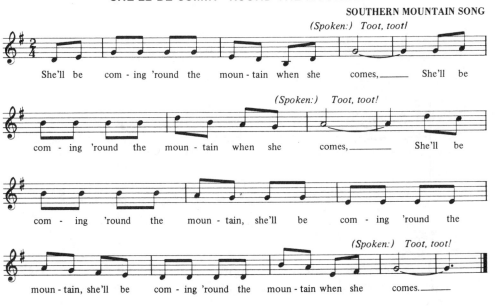

(Spoken:) Toot, toot!

She'll be com-ing 'round the moun-tain when she comes,_____ She'll be

(Spoken:) Toot, toot!

com-ing 'round the moun-tain when she comes,_____ She'll be

com-ing 'round the moun-tain, she'll be com-ing 'round the

(Spoken:) Toot, toot!

moun-tain, she'll be com-ing 'round the moun-tain when she comes._____

Verse 2: She'll be drivin' six white horses
  when she comes ...
Verse 3: Oh, we'll all go out to meet her
  when she comes ...

Verse 4: Then we'll kill the old red rooster

   ...

Verse 5: And we'll all have chicken and
       dumplin's ...

Spoken Words	Motions
Verse 1: Toot, toot!	Pull imaginary train whistle chord for each "toot."
Verse 2: Whoa, back!	Pull on reins.
Verse 3: Hi, there!	Wave hand in greeting.
Verse 4: Cock-a-doodle-doo!	Flap arms like wings.
Verse 5: Yum! Yum!	Rub stomach.

This is a cumulative song, so at the end of each verse, repeat the sound effects and motions of the previous verses. In that way, when the last verse is sung, the words will be: "We'll all have chicken and dumplin's when she comes, Yum, Yum! Cock-a-doodle doo! Hi, there! Whoa back! Toot, toot!"

HOKEY POKEY

SINGING GAME

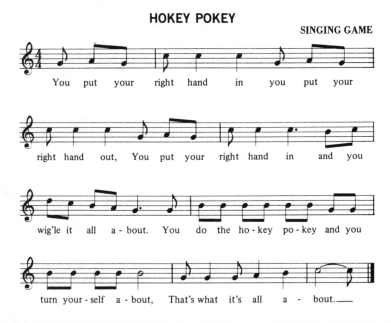

This popular, traditional singing game can be done in circle formation or standing (or sitting) at desks. Suit the actions to the words.

Verse 2: Put your left hand in ...
Verse 3: Put both hands in ...
Verse 4: left foot ...

Verse 5: right foot ...
Verse 6: both feet ...
Additional verses: left shoulder, right
  shoulder, left hip, right hip, whole self.

This game provides an enjoyable way to reinforce the concepts of "left" and "right."

HOW DO YOU PLANT YOUR CABBAGES?

FRENCH FOLK SONG

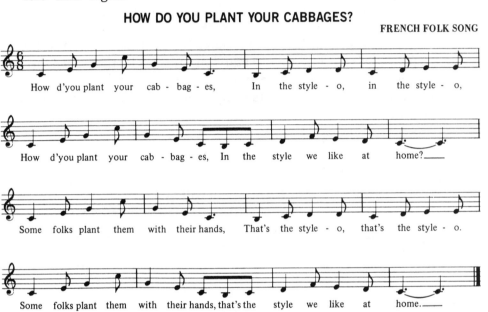

How d'you plant your cab - bag - es, In the style - o, in the style - o,

How d'you plant your cab - bag - es, In the style we like at home?___

Some folks plant them with their hands, That's the style - o, that's the style - o.

Some folks plant them with their hands, that's the style we like at home.___

Have the children suggest different ways to plant the cabbages. They tap the "ground" with the part of the body named.

Verse 2: with the feet
Verse 3: with the heels
Verse 4: with the nose
Verse 5: with the head
Verse 6: with the toes

STAMP YOUR FEET

AMERICAN SINGING GAME

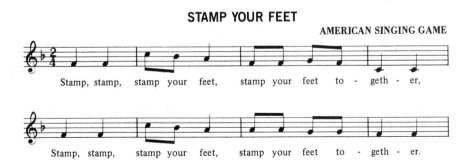

Stamp, stamp, stamp your feet, stamp your feet to - geth - er,

Stamp, stamp, stamp your feet, stamp your feet to - geth - er.

La - la - la - la   la - la - la - la,   la - la - la - la   la,   la,

La - la,   la,   la,   la,   la,   la,   stamp your feet   to - geth - er.

During the second half of the song, the class can continue the stamping. Or, if the children are standing in a circle, they can swing their partners or move around in a circle to the "La-la-la..." Other actions can be substituted for stamping feet. Let the children suggest movements.

> Verse 2: Tap your wrist
> Verse 3: Swing your arms
> Verse 4: Nod your head

THERE'S A LITTLE WHEEL

AMERICAN FOLK SONG

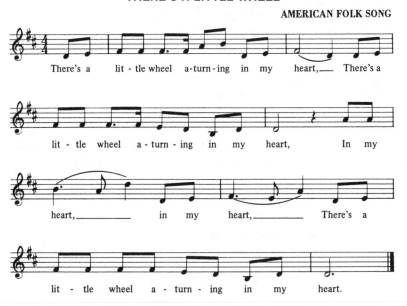

There's a   lit - tle wheel   a - turn - ing   in   my   heart,___   There's a

lit - tle   wheel   a - turn - ing   in   my   heart,   In   my

heart,___   in   my   heart,___   There's   a

lit - tle   wheel   a - turn - ing   in   my   heart.

This is a quiet, restful song and the motions should therefore be done gently.

Words	Motions
There's a little wheel a-turning in my heart.	Wind or turn hands around each other.
In my heart, in my heart....	Clasp both hands to heart.

RHYTHM ACTIVITIES FOR THE HANDICAPPED CHILD

Rhythm activities can be especially valuable for handicapped children. Many of them are very responsive to music and they will be able, with only slight modifications in the activities, to participate together with the other children.

Because partially sighted children frequently have a fear of movement and of bumping into things, be sure that they have plenty of space in which to move freely so that they can comfortably do the same activities used for children with sight.

Children with cerebral palsy or other physical handicaps can relax more to music that allows them to move at a slow pace. Strong, rapid beats would be difficult because they require too much vigorous energy. Also, don't coax these children to respond rhythmically but rather wait for them to join in on their own.

Children who are hard of hearing can sense the vibrations of music through touch. Let them *feel* the rhythms by placing their fingers on the drum or piano as it is being played. They can also learn rhythmic movements by watching and imitating you or the other children in the class. This will help them to become aware of the rhythm inside themselves and they will understand the concepts of meter, duration, and tempo. Clapping and chanting words and rhythms are excellent activities for the hard-of-hearing because these can assist in developing the ability to speak rhythmically and expressively.

Reading
Rhythm Notation

A WORD ABOUT READING RHYTHM NOTATION

Rhythm notation represents, in intellectualized symbolic form, three aspects of time in music. There is the steady underlying pulsation—the rhythm of the beat (/ / / / / / /). There is the (usually) regular rhythm of the meter which divides these pulsations into a pattern of accented and unaccented beats (/ / / | / / | / / , or / / / | / / /). There is the rhythm of the melody—a changing pattern of faster and slower notes (duration) which fit into the underlying pulsation and meter.

The time signature (e.g.: $\frac{2}{2}$, $\frac{2}{4}$, $\frac{3}{4}$) at the beginning of a composition tells us about two of these aspects. The upper number gives the meter—how many counts before the next accented beat. The lower number tells about the steady pulsation—what kind of note gets one count. The measures (the spaces in which the notes appear) are separated by lines, called bars, and each measure contains the number of counts indicated by the time signature. The duration of each tone (the length of time each tone is held) is indicated by notes— various symbols indicating the precise mathematical relationships among the different tones.

Combining these three aspects can result in rhythmic patterns that are easy to understand and perform, or in highly complex rhythms that take years of practice to read at sight or understand. In this chapter, the simplest concepts are given first. For that reason, although this is not always the case in music, we start here with the quarter note as the basic beat that gets one count, and then go on from there. After these simpler rhythms are understood, it isn't as difficult to make the necessary adjustment to learn about more complex rhythms that a slightly more advanced performer would have to know.

The ability to perform rhythmic patterns at sight cannot be developed by reading a chart which gives the mathematical relationships of notes.

What are quarter notes? Walk, stamp, clap, write, read, play, chant, and sing them. Then you will know!

GROUP GAMES AND ACTIVITIES

Clap the Duration

Have the children clap and count out loud quarter notes (♩ ♩ ♩ ♩), half notes (𝅗𝅥 𝅗𝅥 𝅗𝅥 𝅗𝅥), and whole notes (o o o o).

Quarter notes (one count each):   ♩   ♩   ♩   ♩   ♩   ♩
Clap, clap, clap, clap, clap, clap
Say: One, one, one, one, one, one
Half notes (hold each note while you count to 2):

𝅗𝅥   𝅗𝅥   𝅗𝅥   𝅗𝅥

Clap, hold; clap, hold; clap, hold; clap, hold;
Say: One, two; one, two; one, two; one, two
Whole notes (hold each note while you count to 4):

o   o

Clap, wait, wait, wait; clap, wait, wait, wait
Say: One, two, three, four; one, two, three, four

Stamp the Duration

Have the children stamp the quarter, half, and whole notes as they chant the counts.

Walk the Duration

Have the children step to the rhythm of quarter, half, and whole notes. When moving to quarter notes, the pace should be a steady "walk, walk, walk, walk." The pace for half notes should be "step-wait, step-wait, step-wait," and for whole notes, "step-wait-wait-wait, step-wait-wait-wait." Let the children discover that the faster the note, the smaller the movement.

Clap the Duration You See

Write a row of whole, half, and quarter notes in random order on the chalkboard. Reading from left to right, the children clap (or clap-hold) each note for the appropriate number of counts.

You can also teach the dotted half note (𝅗𝅥. = 3 counts) and incorporate this into the activity.

Show the Number of Counts

Tell the children to put their hands behind their backs. When you say, "Go!" they are to hold up the correct number of fingers to show how many counts the named note gets. Call out notes with different durations in random order.

> Whole notes, go! (Children hold up four fingers.)
>
> Quarter notes, go! (Children hold up one finger.)

To add the elements of fun and surprise, keep changing the rate of speed at which you call out the notes and occasionally repeat some of them.

Change the Clap

Have the children start to clap (or stamp) quarter notes. As they do this, call out the name of another kind of note. They should immediately change their clapping to show how many counts the new kind of note gets. Keep changing from whole, to quarter, to half, to dotted half notes, calling out the names of the notes in random order.

Guess Which Note "It" Is

Select a volunteer to be "It." "It" will walk at a rate of speed to demonstrate quarter notes, half notes, or whole notes. The class is to guess what kind of note is being portrayed.

Guess the Note

Play quarter, half, or whole notes on a drum and have the class guess what kind of notes they hear.

Read from the Flash Card

Prepare flash cards on which are written notes of different durations. Start with whole, half, and quarter notes. As the children

learn them, you can add eighth notes (♪♪) and dotted half notes. As each card is held up, the children are to clap (or stamp, or play on rhythm instruments) the kind of note they see.

Play the Measure

Write simple rhythms on the board. Use quarter, half, and whole notes and have the children take turns playing them on the drum. After they have become skillful at playing these simple rhythms, rests and eighth notes can be taught—one concept at a time—and these new symbols incorporated into the rhythms to be performed.

Guess Which Rhythm You Heard

Write three or four brief rhythms on the chalkboard and have the children listen as you play one of them. They are to decide which rhythm you played.

Clap Using Quarter Rests

Teach the quarter note rest (𝄾). Instead of clapping when they see a rest, the children should move their arms apart for one count of silence. Use pictures to help develop the concept, as in the illustration.

After the children have learned to respond to the rest symbol, it can be incorporated into the other group games and paper and pencil activities.

Find Your Rest

Divide the class into teams. Distribute to each team a number of cards, half of which have various notes and half of which have the corresponding rests. At the signal, each child finds and stands next to the partner on his or her team who has the corresponding note or rest. The first team to find partners wins.

Stop and Go

Prepare two traffic signs—a red one saying "STOP" and a green one saying "GO."

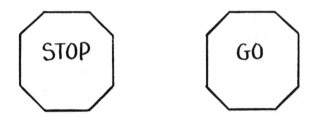

On the back of each Stop sign, write the quarter note rest and write the quarter note on the back of each Go sign. Hold up the Go sign and the children start to clap quarter notes. Hold up the Stop sign and they are silent. Now turn the signs over so that the symbols are shown. When the children see the note on the green sign, they clap. When they see the rest on the red sign, they are silent.

Finally, alternate holding up white cards on which only the music symbols appear. The children clap for the ♩ and are silent for the 𝄽 .

Clap the Notes and Rests

Teach the whole note rest (▬ —silence for four counts) and the half note rest (▬ —silence for two counts). Have the children clap simple rhythms incorporating these symbols. They always move their arms apart for the rests. Then have them play these simple rhythms on the drum or other rhythm instruments. When they come to a rest symbol, they move the hand holding the mallet or beating the instrument away from the instrument.

Chant the Eighth Notes

Teach the eighth notes (♪ ♪ ♪; ♫ ♫). Emphasize that they are so fast that it takes two of them to get one count. Have them chant the word "Running, running, running" as they clap to each syllable.

Run-ning, run-ning, run-ning, run-ning

Chant the Eighth and Quarter Notes

Have the children chant "walk," when they see a quarter note and "running" when they see eighth notes.

Walk, walk, walk, walk, run-ning, run-ning, run-ning, run-ning

Repeat, clapping on each syllable. The eighth notes should be twice as fast as the quarter notes.

Walk, walk, run-ning, walk, walk, run-ning, run-ning, walk

Now have them play these rhythms on various rhythm instruments.

Chant Eighth and Quarter Notes Using Pictures

Other word chants can be developed to help in learning eighth and quarter notes and these can be performed in conjunction with pictures.

1.   Cat,   Cat,   Kit-ty,   Cat

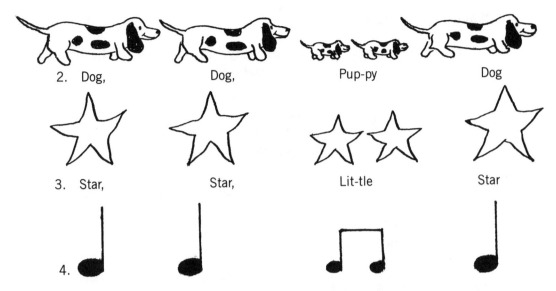

2. Dog,   Dog,   Pup-py   Dog

3. Star,   Star,   Lit-tle   Star

4.

Change Places

Have half of the class clap quarter notes while the other half stamps half notes. When you say, "Change!" those clapping the quarter notes start to stamp half notes and those stamping half notes clap the quarter notes. Change back and forth a number of times.

The same thing can be done with various note combinations—quarter and whole notes, half and whole notes, quarter and eighth notes, half and eighth notes, etc. You can also divide the class into three groups—one clapping quarter notes, one performing half notes by tapping the desks, and one stamping whole notes.

Step Rhythms and Change Places

Several children can step to quarter notes while others walk the half notes. They change movements when you call, "Change." As in the previous activity, different combinations of notes can be used.

Children with physical disabilities who cannot perform these movements can be the conductors who call out the changes.

Move to Two Rhythms at Once

This requires practice to develop coordination. Have the class clap quarter notes. Then have them stamp half notes. See if they can do both of these at the same time. Various other combinations of notes (whole and half notes, quarter and eighth notes, etc.) and movements (tap one type of note with one hand and another with the other hand) can be tried.

Walk the Rhythm You See

Using the notes learned, place rhythm patterns on the board. Have the children chant and clap them:

Walk, walk, run-ning walk, walk, walk, wait

Then, as the rhythms are played on some rhythm instruments by several childen, have other children walk the durations, taking a step on every note. Children walking the rhythmic pattern would squat to indicate a whole note.

Play Duration Race (Board Game)

This can be played by several children. Cut out a circle from oaktag and divide it into sections indicating rests and notes. Attach a black arrow cut from construction paper. A child spins the arrow and then moves his or her disc on the board according to the duration of the note or rest to which the arrow points, as follows:

♩   Move forward one box.

♩   Move forward two boxes.

♩. Move forward three boxes.

○   Move forward four boxes.

♫   Remain in the same box.

𝄽   Go back one box.

▬   Go back two boxes.

▬   Go back four boxes.

THE BOARD

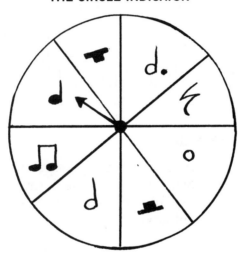

THE CIRCLE INDICATOR

Play Scrambled Measures

Prepare and distribute cards on which incomplete measures are written. At a signal, the children are to find the partner whose card has the number of beats needed to complete his measure. After all the children have found their partners, one pair at a time comes to the front of the room and the class claps the completed rhythms. (See the illustration.)

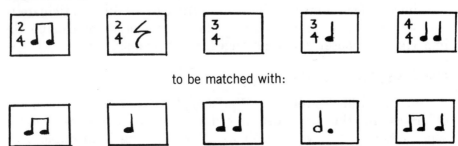

to be matched with:

Play Rhythm Bingo

This can be played by the whole class. Prepare "Bingo" boards on which simple two-, three-, or four-measure rhythms appear. When one of these rhythms is played, the children on whose boards the rhythm appears cover that space with a disc made of construction paper. The first one to accurately cover all the spaces wins.

Fill the Boxes with Notes

Give each child several small empty boxes and many squares of paper on which are drawn notes of various durations. Given a meter ($\frac{2}{4}$, $\frac{3}{4}$, or $\frac{4}{4}$), children are to fill each box with notes so that each box contains a correct combination of notes to add up to the correct number of counts.

Rearrange the Measures

Give several children cards, each of which has a complete measure in a given meter. Have them stand in a row in front of the room as the class claps the resulting rhythm.

Call on one of the children to come to the front of the room and rearrange the children so that they are standing in a different order. Have the class clap the new rhythm. Repeat this several times. (There are some mainstreamed children who may have difficulty reading all but the simplest rhythms. These children can readily participate in this game. They can hold the cards, or one of them can be the important composer who rearranges the rhythms.)

Guess the Meter of the Song

As the children sing a familiar song, have them try to conduct or otherwise find the strong beat in order to determine the meter of the song. When they have decided whether the song is in duple ($\frac{2}{4}$, $\frac{6}{8}$), triple ($\frac{3}{4}$ or $\frac{3}{8}$) or quadruple ($\frac{4}{4}$) meter, let them see a copy of the song in their song books or on a chart so that they can learn whether their decision was correct.

Make a Song Rhythm Chart

As the children learn a new song, have them decide what the meter and tempo are. This information can be put on a chart titled "Songs We Know." One column can show the title of the song, another the meter, and the third, the tempo of the song.

Find a Rhythm Partner

Distribute cards to a number of children, on each of which a one- or two-measure rhythm is drawn. Omit the time signature. For each of these cards, make and distribute another one which will have the corresponding time signature. At the signal, all the children holding cards look for a partner who has either the time signature or the measure which will complete the rhythmic pattern.

Play Rhythm Hop Scotch

Divide the class into teams. On the floor of the classroom or gymnasium, draw a "Rhythm Hop Scotch" game. (See the illustration.) Each square should have a different rhythm. The children take turns throwing a bean bag and then clapping, walking, stamping, or playing on a rhythm instrument the rhythm shown in the box on which the beanbag landed. If the child performs the rhythm accurately, the team gets a point.

Have a Rhythm Spelling Bee

Prepare flash cards showing different rhythms. Each child takes turns clapping a rhythm that is illustrated on a flash card.

Pick a Rhythm

Have various rhythms written on cards. The children take turns coming to the front of the room and picking a card at random. They then play a rhythm instrument or step the selected rhythm while the class decides if the performance is correct. (Again, mainstreamed children having difficulty reading or performing the more complex rhythms can be the ones to hold the cards from which the others select; or, they can select the card to give to the child who will perform the rhythm.)

In a variation of this game, a child can select a rhythm and then the whole class can clap it.

Write as Many Measures as You Can (Team Game)

Divide the class into two teams. At the signal, every child tries to think of and write as many measures in a given meter ($\frac{2}{4}$, $\frac{3}{4}$, $\frac{4}{4}$) as he or she can, using the notes and rests learned (whole, half, quarter, eighth, dotted half notes and whole, half, quarter rests). When they have finished, check the work. The team with the most correct measures wins.

Play Rhythm Spin-the-Arrow

Prepare a "Spin-the-Arrow" game using a sheet of oaktag or heavy cardboard for the board and black construction paper for the arrow. Children take turns spinning the arrow and performing the rhythm to which the arrow points.

Pantomime Rhythm Activities; Find Their Note Durations

Have the children make a list of activities or things in their environment that have a steady, recurring beat (e.g., rain falling, running, ice skating, walking, carrying a heavy load, clock ticking, church bells ringing, treadmill turning). Have them pantomine these movements. Then, as a drum accompanies their movement, let them decide whether the beat can be represented by quarter notes, half notes, whole notes, or eighth notes. Next to each item on the list, the children write the kind of note they have determined represents its rhythm.

Running

Walking

Church bells chiming

Ice skating

Rain falling

Clock ticking

Carrying a heavy load

Treadmill turning

Clap Three Kinds of Rhythm

Write a rhythmic pattern on the chalkboard and divide the class into three groups. The first group plays the steady pulsation of the quarter note beat on rhythm sticks. The second group stamps only on the first count of each measure—the rhythm of the accented beat. The third group claps the rhythm of the melody—the changing patterns of duration.

The most challenging of these three activities is the clapping of the changing durations. Children who have difficulty learning the more complex rhythmic patterns can enjoy this activity as they play the steady quarter note beat on rhythm sticks or other instruments.

Note Relay Race: Fix the Mistake

Divide the class into two teams. On the chalkboard, write two series of measures, one series for each team. Have as many measures as there are children participating. Each measure should have one error in the rhythm.

At the signal, the first child on each team runs to the board, looks for and corrects an error in any of the measures. When finished, he or she runs back to the team and the next child has a turn to find and fix an error. This continues until one team has found and corrected the errors in all the measures.

Note Relay Race: Write a Measure

This game is similar to the "Fix the Mistake Relay Race." In this activity, each child on the team is to run to the board and write a measure in an indicated meter. The first team to be finished wins the relay race.

Write the Rhythm of the Name

The children should have had the experience of clapping and chanting their names and should have developed some familiarity with rhythmic notation.

Call on a volunteer to print his or her name on the chalkboard and divide it into syllables. Have the children clap the name and decide which syllables should be represented rhythmically by eighth notes and which should be represented by other notes.

Find the Eighth Notes

Have a child play a steady beat on the drum. These are the quarter notes. The other children try to "hear" the eighth notes "inside" the quarter notes. As soon as they are able to feel two beats to each one being played on the drum, they start to clap the eighth notes.

Let several children take turns establishing the quarter note beat.

Play Rhythm Duets

Prepare a chart showing two rhythms to be performed at the same time, as follows:

Divide the class in half. One group claps the top rhythm while the other group stamps or slaps thighs to the second rhythm.

Read Two Rhythms at the Same Time

Prepare a chart showing two rhythms to be performed at the same time. Have the children play the top rhythm by tapping it out with one hand on their desks. They then tap the lower rhythm with the other hand and finally, tap both rhythms at the same time. (This activity requires a good deal of muscle control and coordination.) Start with very simple and repetitious patterns and gradually make the rhythm combination more challenging.

PAPER AND PENCIL ACTIVITIES

Write Rows of Notes

Have the children write a row of quarter notes and under each one place the figure "1" to indicate the duration of the quarter note.

QUARTER NOTES

Do the same thing for half and then whole notes. Later, when the children are very familiar with these, have them write a row of dotted half notes.

HALF NOTES

WHOLE NOTES

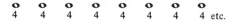

DOTTED HALF NOTES

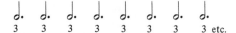

Write the Number of Counts

Give the children work sheets on which whole, half, quarter, and dotted half notes are written in random order. Under each note, the child writes the number of counts each note receives.

Find the Walking Notes

Give the children work sheets on which short rhythm phrases appear. Have them circle all the quarter notes they can find.

Find the Waiting Notes

Have the children circle, using any color they choose, all the half notes in several rhythm phrases.

Draw the Bar Lines

Distribute work sheets; have the children draw bar lines to form measures. They place the bar lines so that each box or measure contains notes whose duration adds up to the number of counts indicated by the time signature at the beginning of the rhythmic pattern.

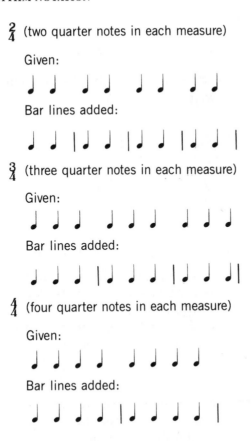

$\frac{2}{4}$ (two quarter notes in each measure)

Given:

Bar lines added:

$\frac{3}{4}$ (three quarter notes in each measure)

Given:

Bar lines added:

$\frac{4}{4}$ (four quarter notes in each measure)

Given:

Bar lines added:

As children learn dotted half notes, eighth notes, and rests, these should be incorporated into the rhythms.

Write Your Own Measures: Use Quarter Notes

Have the children write the correct number of quarter notes to achieve the indicated meter in each measure.

Given:

$\frac{2}{4}$ | | | |

Answer:

$\frac{2}{4}$

Given:

$\frac{3}{4}$ | | | |

Answer:

After the written work is done, have the children clap and count the measures they have written.

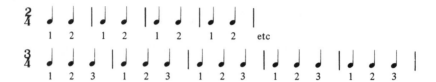

Write Your Own Measures Using Different Kinds of Notes

Given a meter, have the children write several measures using quarter and half notes. As each new kind of note is learned—whole notes, eighth notes, dotted half notes—have them write measures incorporating these notes. Select volunteers to write their measures on the chalkboard and have the class clap them.

Add the Missing Note

Give the children work sheets showing measures, each of which needs another note to add up to the correct meter. Have them fill in the beats by adding *one* (and only one) note.

Find the Rhythm Errors

Distribute work sheets on which rhythmic patterns are written. Some of the measures should be correct and some should contain errors. Have the children find the errors and add or subtract whatever notes are necessary to achieve the correct rhythm.

Given:

Answer:

Change the Notes to Rests

Children are given work sheets showing rhythms with some of the notes circled. They rewrite the rhythms, changing the designated notes to rests of the same duration. They then clap the rhythms.

Given:

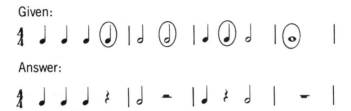

Answer:

Change the Rests to Notes

Given measures with some rests circled, the children change these rests to notes of the same duration.

Given:

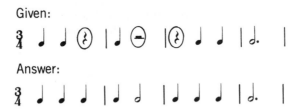

Answer:

Guess the Meter

Play a series of rhythmic patterns on a drum, exaggerating the accent on the first beat. The children are to guess what the meter is and indicate their answer by circling the appropriate time signature on their work sheets.

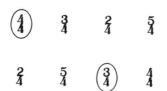

Find the Meter

Give the children work sheets on which a number of rhythmic patterns are shown. Omit the time signatures. The children are to decide what the correct time signatures are and write them in the correct places.

Match the Notes and the Rests

Give the children work sheets on which are written notes and rests in any position on the page. Have them draw lines connecting the rest to the note having the same duration. (See the illustration.)

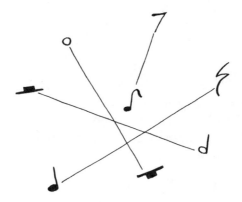

Find the Same Rhythm

On a work sheet, have several series of measures, two of which in each series will have the same rhythm. The children draw circles around those rhythms which are the same. They then try to clap all of the rhythms.

Find the Correct Measure

Prepare a work sheet showing a series of rhythms in each of which only one rhythm is correct. The children find the correct measure and a volunteer is selected to play it on the rhythm instrument of his or her choice.

Complete the Measures

On a work sheet, write a column of measures which need additional notes to add up to the indicated time signature. The children are to select the notes written in a second column which could complete the measures.

Draw a Notes Chart

Each child receives a sheet of construction paper on which he or she draws the following diagram:

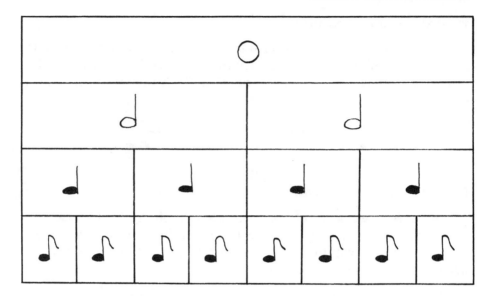

The various fractional relationships can be seen from the diagram.

Make Note Cards

Starting with note relationship diagrams drawn on heavy construction paper, the children cut up the relationship diagrams so that the segments representing each note are in proportion to the duration of the note. They can then use these cards to figure out combinations of notes which will add up to the number of counts indicated by a time signature.

The mathematical relationship of notes is an intellectual concept which can best be understood only after many experiences with rhythms. Children should clap, stamp, chant, walk, and play rhythms and have many experiences with activities described in this chapter.

Match the Picture to the Notes

Distribute work sheets with two columns. In one column, have stick figures showing people involved in various activities. In the second column, show rhythmic patterns which can illustrate the activities. The children match the rhythms with the activities. See the illustration on page 107.

Find Rhythms in Music Scores

Distribute copies of familiar songs and let the children look for

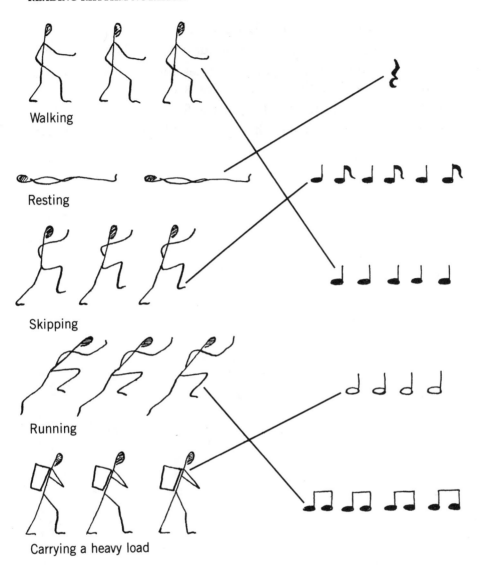

Walking

Resting

Skipping

Running

Carrying a heavy load

and identify various aspects of rhythm. Have them try to answer appropriate questions about each song, such as the following:

1. How many counts are there in each measure?
2. How many measures are there on the first line?
3. Measure three has a twin. Can you find another measure with the same rhythm? If so, draw a circle around it.

4. Color in the whole notes. Use any color you like.

5. Find the quarter note rests and put a check above each one.

6. The first line has mostly quarter notes and half notes. Can you find another line that has the same kinds of notes?

7. Which line is faster, the first or the fourth?

8. Draw a diagram to show how you would conduct this song.

LEARNiNg
HOW TO LiSTEN TO MUSiC

When you walk down a city street, you see and hear youths pass by carrying blaring transistor radios. When you ride in an elevator or shop in a department store, you hear "Muzak." We are so surrounded by sound and so inundated by "music" that we stop listening.

The games and activities in this chapter will help to develop—or to restore—the skills and habits of listening to music with sensitivity, pleasure, awareness, and concentration. Children can learn to listen attentively. They can experience pleasurable active participation while listening—moving, creating, playing instruments. The two are not mutually exclusive; there are times when they can just listen and times when they can dance or draw or act to music. In all cases, the goal is to develop awareness of what they hear, and to enjoy listening.

Here are a few hints:

1. If you want to engage the children in any of the suggested activities, have them first listen to the music to hear the particular facet they are exploring.

2. Many of the suggested recordings are suitable for all grades. They can be played for children in early childhood classes and in the concert hall for adults. Where the grade levels are given in the lists of recordings (for the *Adventures in Music* series), it is only for the purposes of convenience because that is the way the series is divided. There is *no such thing* as fourth grade, third grade, sixth grade, or first grade music. There is beautiful music, or expressive, or harsh, or lively, or quiet, or interesting—or dull—music. Play any of the compositions you like for any grade. It is what you *do* with them—how you will engage the children in activities suitable for their age, intel-

ligence, and levels of musical and social sophistication—that will vary.

3. Start with shorter works of a few minutes duration and, as the children develop the attention span required for listening, gradually increase the length of the compositions. This is not necessarily related to age or grade level. The more experience children have just *listening,* the longer they will be able to listen. Sixth grade children whose musical backgrounds have been lacking might not have better listening skills than six-year-olds who have had many opportunities for perceptive listening.

4. Listen together with the children. A teacher who marks papers, reads, or engages in conversation with colleagues while music is being played, is hardly likely to encourage good listening habits in his or her pupils. In other words, try to "look the way the music sounds."

LISTENING FOR TIMBRE
(TONE QUALITY)

Play "Who Was That?"

Go around the class taping the voices—singing or speaking—of a number of children in the class. Tell the class to listen carefully because later in the day, they will try to identify the voices. Several hours later, play back the tape and let the children try to guess whose voices they hear.

Play "Where Is the Sound?"

Have several children volunteer to stand in back of the room where they will not be seen by the others. As the rest of the children cover their eyes, point to one of the volunteers who will read a sentence written on the chalkboard. Have the class try to guess whose voice was heard.

Play "What Did You Hear Now?"

Have a "Surprise Box" into which several rhythm instruments are placed. As the children keep their eyes closed, play one of the instruments and have them guess which one you played. If they recognize the sound, they raise their hands. Call on one of the children and if he or she guesses correctly, he or she becomes "It" and has the chance to select the next instrument.

Start with instruments that are easily distinguishable (e.g., drum, maracas, triangle, rhythm sticks) and then, when the children are more familiar with them, choose instruments that are more closely related in timbre (tone quality).

One of the more challenging combinations could be triangle, finger cymbals, melody (song) bells, Swiss hand-held bells, and cymbals.

Locate the Sound

Give four or five children different rhythm instruments and station them in different parts of the classroom. Have the rest of the children cover their eyes and then point to one of the children holding an instrument. This child plays the instrument and the class tries to locate the direction from which the sounds are coming.

Locate the Moving Sound

As the children keep their eyes closed, play a rhythmic pattern on the drum. Have them point, eyes still closed, to the direction from which the sound is coming. Keep changing your position in the room as you play the drum. The children are to point to the changing location of the drum.

Find the Instrument That Does Not Belong

Have pictures of instruments which produce their sounds in the same way. Include one picture of an instrument which belongs to a different family. The children decide which one does not belong.

> Have pictures of a clarinet, trombone,
> flute, recorder, and violin.
> Answer: The violin does not belong. It is a
> string instrument. The others are
> wind instruments.

Match the Pictures with the Sounds

Have a series of large pictures or posters of different instruments and display them in front of the room. Play brief excerpts of music and call on a volunteer to come to the front of the room to select the picture of the instrument heard. Continue this until excerpts illustrating all of the pictured instruments are heard.

Find the Family of the Instruments

Have a list of instruments or a work sheet showing pictures of the instruments. Next to each, have the children write the name of the family (string, woodwind, brass, percussion) to which the instrument belongs.

Make an Instrument Bulletin Board

Prepare a bulletin board or chart showing four sections labeled String, Woodwind, Brass, and Percussion. The children draw or bring in pictures of instruments and paste them on the appropriate part of the chart.

Play the Instrument You See

Hold up pictures of instruments, calling out the names. As each picture is displayed, the children make believe that they are playing the instrument, pantomiming the required motions.

Play the Instrument Names

After the children have become somewhat familiar with the instruments, have a series of cards with the names of the instruments. As you hold up the cards at random, the children imitate playing the instrument named.

Show Which Instrument You Hear

Distribute pictures of a number of instruments to some children and to other children, cards on which are written the names of these instruments. Play a recording of music illustrating one of these instruments. The children holding the picture of the instrument or the card with its name come to the front of the room and show them to the class. Repeat the activity a few times using very brief recordings illustrating some of the other instruments.

Find Your Instrument Partner (Team Game)

Divide the class into two teams. Give half of the children on each team pictures of instruments and the other half cards with the names of the instruments. At the signal, each child finds the partner on his or her own team who has the matching picture or name. The first team to find its partners wins.

Have an Instrument Scrap Book

Keep a large "Musical Instruments" scrapbook, scissors, and paste in the "Music Corner. "During free time, those children who draw or find pictures of musical instruments or of musicians playing instruments can paste them into the scrapbook for the rest of the class to enjoy. Suggest to the children that they can find pictures in newspapers or magazines, but that they should first obtain permission to cut them out.

Match the Instrument to Its Name

Have a work sheet showing a number of pictures of instruments in one column, and in the second column, names of the instruments. The children match the instruments with the correct name. (See the illustration.)

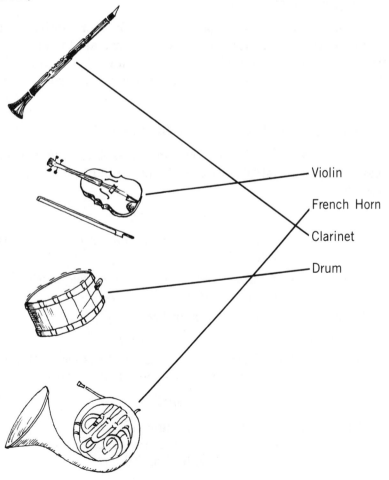

Violin

French Horn

Clarinet

Drum

Guess the Instrument, "Who Am I?"

Play a "Twenty Questions" type of game. Present a series of hints and see if the children can guess the name of the instrument being described. This can be done orally or a work sheet can be prepared.

1. I can play all kinds of music—folk songs, classical music, or "Rock."
2. Many people use me to accompany singing.
3. I am a string instrument.
4. I have six strings.
5. I don't have a bow.

Answer: The guitar.

Invite Guest Artists

Some of your pupils may have relatives or family friends who play instruments. Invite them to visit your class to demonstrate and play their instruments. If any of the youngsters in your class or in other classes play, arrange to have them perform for the other children.

Recordings That Illustrate the Instruments

You probably have your own favorites, but here are some good examples to illustrate different instruments of the band and orchestra.

Woodwinds

Piccolo: "Chinese Dance" from *The Nutcracker Suite,* by Tchaikowsky.

Flute: "Les Mirlitons" from *The Nutcracker Suite.* Bird from *Peter and the Wolf,* by Prokofiev.

Clarinet: "Cat" from *Peter and the Wolf.*

Oboe: "Duck" from *Peter and the Wolf.*

Bassoon: "Grandfather" from *Peter and the Wolf.* "Broom" music from *The Sorcerer's Apprentice,* by Dukas.

Brass

Trumpet: Any recording of bugle calls.
The trumpet call from the last section of the Overture to *William Tell,* by Rossini.

Trombone: "Ride of the Valkyries," by Wagner.

French Horn: "Wolf," from *Peter and the Wolf.*

String

Violin "Peter" from *Peter and the Wolf.*
> Square dance music illustrating the "fiddle."

Cello: "The Swan" from *Carnival of the Animals* by Saint-Saëns.

Harp: Introduction to "Waltz of the Flowers" from *The Nutcracker Suite.*

Double Bass: "The Elephant," from *Carnival of the Animals.*

Percussion

Xylophone: "Skeleton" music from *Danse Macabre* by Saint-Saëns.

Bells: *1812* Overture by Tchaikowsky.

Drums: African drumming (including recordings by Olatunji). Marches by Sousa.

Several compositions contain narrations which introduce the instruments as they are heard. These include *Tubby the Tuba,* by Kleinsinger, *Peter and the Wolf,* by Prokofiev, and *A Young Person's Guide to the Orchestra,* by Britten. The last named work would be suitable for older children but because of its length, it might be a good idea to play, at other times, the music illustrating the instruments of different families as they are heard on the recording. It would also be helpful to have pictures or posters illustrating the instruments as they are heard.

LEARNING ABOUT DYNAMICS

Show the Need for Dynamics

Start to read a story in a dull monotone without varying the intensity of your voice or accentuating any words or syllables. Ask the children if they like the way you are reading. The discussion should bring out the need for variety in voice quality and the realization that some words and ideas should be louder, or softer. Relate that concept to the need for variety of dynamics in music.

Experiment with Dynamic Intensity

Write a simple sentence on the board. Have the class read it, emphasizing different words and changing inflections and degrees of loudness and softness.

> Johnny ran to school.
> *Johnny* ran to school.
> Johnny *ran* to school.
> Johnny ran to *school*!
> *Johnny* ran to school?
> Whispered: Johnny ran to school.
> Johnny *ran* to school?

Have them notice the differences in nuance and mood created by the different interpretations of the sentence.

Experiment with Dynamic Intensity in Music

Tell the children that you are going to sing a lullabye for them. Have them put their heads on their desks, close their eyes, and make themselves as comfortable as possible.

Start to sing a lullabye in a harsh, very loud voice. Many of the children will probably start to laugh. They will tell you that a lullabye should not be so loud. Try singing the song at different degrees of intensity until the children decide which one is most appropriate. Then ask if it *does* make a difference whether music is loud or soft.

This activity can make the children aware of the need for and the effects of dynamics in music.

Learn the Symbols for Loud and Soft

Teach the terms *forte* (*f* — loud) and *piano* (*p* — soft). Clap a rhythm or play it on a drum and have the children imitate you. Write *f* and *p* on the board or on two cards. As the class continues to clap the rhythm, hold up one of the cards (or point to the symbol). If the card has the symbol *f*, the children's clapping is loud; if it has the symbol *p*, the clapping is soft.

Tiptoe and Stamp

Play examples of music that have varying dynamics. You can use recordings or play rhythms on a drum, or improvise at the piano. Select a group of children to move to the music. When the music is *forte,* they stamp as they walk. When the music is *piano,* they walk on tiptoe.

Dance with Fingers and Hands

Play examples of music that have varied dynamics. When the music is loud, the children tap on their hands. When the music is soft, they "dance" with their fingers, moving them lightly on their desks in time to the music.

Express Dynamics Through Art

Have the children listen to examples of soft music and of loud music. Select compositions that have different moods and obvious dynamics. Tell them to listen quietly and see how the music makes them feel or of what it makes them think.

After that, distribute large sheets of drawing paper and crayons and have the children label one side of the paper *p* and the other side *f.* Tell them that, as they hear the soft music again, they should draw on the side labeled *p* any design or picture, using any colors that the music suggests to them. They then do the same thing for the loud music, drawing on the side labeled *f.*

You may find that some of the children will not have finished their pictures when the recordings end and will want to hear the music again—and again. This is fine. At the same time that they are expressing their feelings about the music, they are becoming familiar with the music itself.

Some children may, at first, be inhibited and unable to draw to the music. You can help by giving such suggestions as, "Move your hands in the air to the music and make believe you are holding a crayon," or "Should you press lightly or hard for the loud music?"

If any of the children *don't* want to draw, let them just listen quietly.

When the drawings are done, select some of them and show them to the class. Hide the symbols *p* and *f* and have the children guess which picture represents which symbol. You will find that, in most cases, the differences in the drawings are obvious.

Express Dynamics Using Rhythm Instruments

Play music that has sharp distinctions between loud and soft sections. Let the children listen and determine which parts are *p,* which *f, ff (fortissimo*—very loud), and which *pp (pianissimo*—very soft). Distribute several rhythm instruments and have the children decide which ones would provide an appropriate accompaniment for each section. Finger cymbals, triangles, and a delicate tapping of rhythm sticks or tone blocks, for example, might be suitable for the *p* sections, while strong cymbal crashes and drum beats might play along when the music is *ff.*

Play "Lullabye and Wake Up"

This activity is a good one for little children. Tape portions of music illustrating *p* and *f* (e.g., a lullabye and a march). When the soft music is played, the children put their heads on their desks and pretend to sleep. When the loud music is played, they stand, stretching. Alternate this several times.

Little and Big Windmills

This is another movement activity to illustrate *p* and *f,* which is suitable for young children. Play the taped portions of music. When the music is soft, the children gently move their hands like windmills, winding and turning them around each other. When the music is loud, they move their hands vigorously. It is important, however, that they express *f* by making larger movements, not by making faster movements. *Forte* is achieved by an increased amount of intensity and strength, not by speeding.

Move the Way the Music Sounds

Have the children move in any way they wish to express loud and soft music. Music can be supplied by recordings, playing the drum, or improvising at the piano. Try these different combinations:

Fast and loud *(Allegro e forte)*—strong, quick movements.

Fast and soft *(Allegro e piano)*—quick, gentle movements.

Slow and loud *(Largo e forte)*—strong, slow movements.

Slow and soft *(Largo e piano)*—gentle, slow movements.

Change without warning from one kind of playing to another to encourage the children to listen carefully.

Respond to Flash Cards

Prepare flash cards, one for each dynamics symbol the children learn. They could include *pp—pianissimo,* very soft; *p—piano,* soft;

mp—mezzo piano, medium soft; *mf—mezzo forte,* medium loud; *f—*

forte, loud; *ff—fortissimo,* very loud; ⟨———————⟩ *—crescendo,* grad-

ually become louder; ⟨———————⟩ *—decrescendo,* gradually become

softer.

Start to clap a rhythmic pattern and have the children imitate you. As you show the flash cards, they continue clapping the rhythm pattern, changing the degree of loudness or softness according to the symbol shown. *The clapping should not get faster as it gets louder.* This activity is suitable for *all* grade levels.

Follow the Dynamics Instructions

Write the dynamics symbols on the board and distribute rhythm instruments. Select one child to be the conductor and another to make up a rhythmic pattern. As the musicians play their rhythm instruments, the conductor points to the different symbols and they respond by varying the dynamics level at which they play.

Use Movement to Express Crescendo and Decrescendo

Teach the children the terms *crescendo* ⟨———————⟩ , gradually become louder) and *decrescendo* ⟨———————⟩ , gradually become softer.) Have them "make themselves as small as possible," huddling close to the floor or to their desks, arms covering heads, heads dropped towards their chests. Play music with a strong *crescendo.* You can do this through piano improvisation, drum rhythms, or suitable recordings.

As the music becomes louder, the children gradually straighten up and stretch their arms out to the sides, making themselves "bigger and bigger." To express *decrescendo,* a drum, piano, or any suitable recording is played and the movement is reversed. The children make themselves "smaller" until they return to their original positions.

Draw to Illustrate *Crescendo* and *Decrescendo*

The children start to draw any design they would like on the left side of a sheet of paper (e.g., wavy lines, squares, circles, vertical lines, squiggles). Play music that has a definite *crescendo* and, as the music becomes louder and louder, the children draw the same design (going from left to right on the paper), each time making the design a little bit larger. To illustrate *decrescendo,* start with a large diagram and repeat over and over, each time making the design smaller and smaller. (See the illustration.)

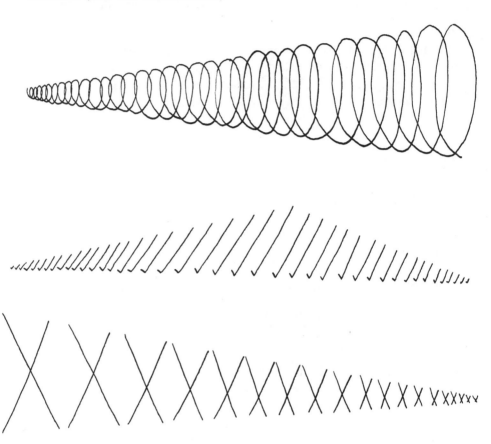

Use Dynamics with Word Chants

After the children have developed some word chants on a selected theme, divide the class into groups—each one to chant a different sentence or phrase. Have one child be the conductor who will point to different dynamics symbols to indicate how loud or soft the chant should be.

Listen to the Surprise

Tell the children the story of the second movement of Haydn's *Surprise Symphony* (partially based on fact).

Franz Joseph Haydn was a famous composer who lived about two hundred years ago, when George Washington was alive. (If possible, show a picture of Haydn.) In those days, musicians worked for great princes, kings or dukes, composing and playing music for them and for their friends and relatives. Haydn worked for Prince Esterhazy. Every day, he would compose music and rehearse it with the musicians and then they would play it at night, after dinner.

After a big meal, at which all the guests had eaten a *lot,* they all sat around in comfortable chairs listening to the music. What do you think could have happened when the musicians began to play the slow, soft music and everyone felt so comfortable, full and lazy? (The class should be able to guess, "They fell asleep.")

Haydn didn't like this. After all, he had worked hard to compose the music and the musicians had worked hard practicing all day. And here, everyone was asleep! So this is what Haydn did when the musicians reached the slow, soft part.

At this point in the story, tell the children to pretend that they are Prince Esterhazy's guests. They are to make themselves as comfortable as possible, close their eyes, and pretend to be asleep.

Play the main theme of the second movement of Haydn's Symphony in G Major, No. 94 *(Surprise).* Turn down the volume so that the music is especially soft. When the sudden *ff* chord is reached at the end of the theme, turn up the volume. The response will undoubtedly be laughter and surprise.

Now, finish the story.

That's what happened to the prince and the princess and to all the lords and ladies. They realized that Haydn had played a joke on them and from then on, this work has been called the *Surprise Symphony.*

You'll find that the children will love to play this game many times, pretending to be asleep and waking, startled, at the chord crash.

Play the "Surprise"

Teach the meaning of "accent" in music—a sudden, loud sound (indicated by $\overset{>}{\mathsf{p}}$ $\overset{\wedge}{\mathsf{p}}$ $\overset{'}{\mathsf{p}}$ or *sf*—sforzando).

Distribute rhythm instruments to a number of children and tell them that they are to play the "accent" of Haydn's *Surprise Symphony*. Play the recording of the main theme of the second movement (with which the children should be familiar) and have them all wait, instruments ready. At the "Surprise" chord, they all bang, crash, shake, or hit their instruments.

A number of functions are served by this activity; the children are developing control of their movements, they are learning to listen intently; they are memorizing the theme of Haydn's *Surprise Symphony* so that later, when they hear the movement in its entirety, they will be able to understand the variations: they are experiencing happy associations with good music; and they are practicing the concept of accent.

Decide How the Song Should Be Sung

After the class has learned a song, let them try singing it using various interpretations—sweetly, softly, vigorously, loudly, using echo effects, gradually getting softer or louder. Have them decide which way they like it best.

Have a "Songs We Know" Chart

Make a "Songs We Know" chart. The children can indicate information about the songs' dynamics. As they learn new concepts of music, these can be added. Eventually, the chart could indicate the composer, meter, tempo, country of origin, key (if they learn this), note on which the song starts, note on which it ends, dynamics, and form.

Create Your Own Dynamics Symbols

Suggest to the pupils that they make up their own signs for "soft," "loud," "get loud," "very soft," "get soft." Let them show some of the signs to their classmates and see if the other children can guess what the symbols represent. (See the illustration.)

Find Dynamics Levels in the Environment

Take the children for a walk and have them listen to sounds in their environment. Have them classify them according to how loud or soft they are. When they return to the classroom, have them list these sounds (and others they can think of) and next to each one, write the dynamics symbol that would best describe the sound.

> Airplane overhead—*ff*
>
> Mouse squeaking—*p*
>
> Tiptoe—*pp*
>
> Stamping—*f*
>
> Thunder nearby—*ff*
>
> People talking—*mp* or *mf*
>
> Car going away— $\diagdown$
>
> Bus coming closer— $\diagup$
>
> Whispering—*pp*

Recordings to Illustrate Dynamics:

p; pp: "The Swan" from *Carnival of the Animals* by Saint-Saëns, in *Adventures in Music* series, RCA Records; Grade 3, Volume 2.

"Barcarolle," by Offenbach, in *Adventures in Music,* Grade 3, Volume 1.

"The Snow Is Dancing," by Debussy, in *Adventures in Music,* Grade 3, Volume 1.

First movement, "Moonlight" Sonata, by Beethoven.

Second movement, Piano Concerto in C, by Mozart.

f: ff: "Ride of the Valkyries," by Wagner
"Lesginka," from *Gayne* Suite, by Khachaturian.
"Sabre Dance," from *Gayne* Suite by Khachaturian.
A Sousa March.

crescendo and/or decrescendo: "Hall of the Mountain King," from *Peer Gynt* Suite by Grieg, *Adventures in Music,* Grade 3, Volume 2 ($\diagup$)

"Morning" from *Peer Gynt* Suite by Grieg. ($\diagup$)

"Bydlo," from *Pictures at an Exhibition,* by Moussorgsky, *Adventures in Music,* Grade 2, Volume 1; a cart drawn by an ox approaches from a distance and then gradually goes away. ($\Longleftarrow\Longrightarrow$).

"Parade," from *Divertissement,* by Ibert, *Adventures in Music,* Grade 1, Volume 1; a parade comes closer and then moves away ($\Longleftarrow\Longrightarrow$).

Strong contrasts in dynamics: "Fairies and Giants," from *Wand of Youth* Suite No. 1, by Elgar *Adventures in Music,* Grade 3, Volume 1.

Toccata, from Toccata and Fugue in d Minor by Bach; originally written for organ, the orchestral arrangement by Stokowski may be more obvious to beginning listeners.

"Baba Yaga," from *Pictures at an Exhibition,* by Moussorgsky.

"Ritual Fire Dance," by De Falla.

Selections from *Carmen* Suite, by Bizet, on *Conduct Your Own Orchestra,* Golden Records 47.

Selection from *Romeo and Juliet,* by Tchaikowsky, on *Conduct Your Own Orchestra,* Golden Records, GLP 47.

LEARNING ABOUT MUSICAL FORM

Find the Breathing Places in the Words of a Song
(Introducing the Concept of Phrase)

Recite the words of a familiar song without pausing for breath at commas or periods. Ask the class what was wrong. Recite the words again and have the children raise their hands every time you come to the end of a sentence or should take a breath.

Find the Phrases

Sing a song without pausing or stopping for breath. Have the class tell you how to improve the performance. Repeat the song and have the children raise their hands when you should breathe or when you come to the end of a sentence or "musical idea."

Have them sing the song with you, noting where they take their breaths. (Good songs for this activity are "Home on the Range" and "Oh, What a Beautiful Morning.") Explain to them that they have sung with phrases and that a phrase is like a musical sentence.

Walk the Phrase

Have the children sing a lyrical song and select volunteers to walk to the song. They start to walk in one direction and when the phrase comes to an end, they turn and walk in the other direction. This is repeated throughout the song, the children turning and move to the phrase walking in another direction each time a phrase ends.

Move to the Phrase

Several other movement activities can be done to develop the feeling for a phrase:

1. Have the children stand in a circle holding hands. They walk around clockwise as the music starts and change direction each time a phrase starts.
2. The children can stand or remain seated and sway, arms overhead, to the phrase, changing their direction for each new phrase.

Circle the Phrase

Give the class copies of the score of a familiar song. Have them sing it, noting where the phrases should occur—where they breathe or where the musical idea ends. Have them sing it again and this time, as they do, have them draw curved arcs above the words and music to show where the different phrases begin and end:

AMERICA

My coun - try 'tis of thee, Sweet land of lib - er - ty,

Of thee I sing. Land where my fa - thers died, Land of the

Pil - grim's pride, From ev - 'ry moun - tain side, Let free - dom ring.

Draw Diagrams to Show ABA Form

Play a composition in ABA form. In ABA form, there is a first melody or musical section (A), a contrasting section or musical idea (B), and then a repetition of the first section or idea (A). Ask the children to decide, as they listen, what kind of design they could draw to illustrate each part of the music. Distribute drawing paper and crayons and have the children divide the page into three vertical sections.

Play the music again. As the A section is heard, the pupils draw a design in the first column. When the music changes and the second section starts, they immediately start to draw a different design, using different colors, in the second column. When the A section is repeated, they draw the same design in the third column that they did in the first.

Tell them that the first column representing the first part of the music is called A. You should be able to elicit from them that the second column represents B and the third is A again. Inform them that a song or other musical composition is frequently made up of a three-part design called ABA form.

You may have to play the composition more than once to enable the children to finish their drawings. This would have the added advantage of giving them the opportunity to become very familiar with the music. Any child who does not want to draw can just listen quietly to the music.

Display the drawings when the children have finished them and have labeled the columns ABA. (See the illustration.)

A   B   A

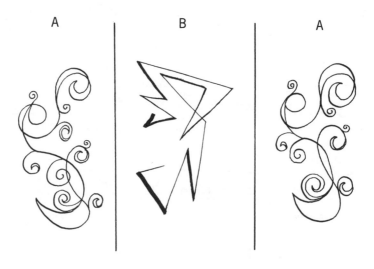

Use Rhythm Band for ABA Form

Play a composition having ABA form. Have the children decide which rhythm instruments would be best to accompany the A and which would be best for the B section. Distribute those instruments and have the children play along at the right times—first the A instruments, then the B, then the A again.

Dance ABA Form

Play a composition having ABA form. Have two groups of children—the A group and the B group. Have each group develop a dance suitable for their section of the music. Play the composition again. First the A group dances, then the B group, then the A group again. Children who are unable to participate because of physical disabilities can accompany the music using rhythm instruments.

Find ABA Form in Your Favorite Songs and Music

After the children have become familiar with ABA form, they can start to analyze the songs they sing, listening and studying the music scores to find where repetitions or changes occur. Encourage them to bring from home recordings or tapes of their favorite songs and music that could illustrate ABA form.

Count the Number of Times You Hear the Theme

Play a composition in which the same melody (theme) keeps recurring. (A rondo is a musical form in which the same melody is repeated, interspersed with other themes or melodies.) Distribute several cards on which the word "THEME" appears. Every time the theme is played, one of the children holding a card stands. When the music is finished, the class counts the number of children standing to learn how many times the theme was played.

Diagram a Rondo

Prepare a series of shapes cut from felt—triangles, squares, circles, rectangles. Label all of one kind of shape, "A: Main Theme." Label all of another shape, "B," another , "C," etc. Distribute the cutouts and play the main theme of a rondo. When the main theme is heard, one of the pupils holding a shape labeled "Main Theme" brings the shape to the front of the room and places it on the felt board. When the second melody is heard, a child holding a "B" shape places it next to the first one. When the third melody is played, the one holding a shape labeled "C" places that on the board. Whenever the main theme is heard, it will be represented by the same shape as the first one.

Play the complete rondo. The final diagram (depending on the composition played) should look something like the illustration.

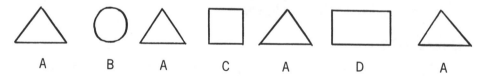

| A | B | A | C | A | D | A |

Play a Rondo

Have the children decide which rhythm instruments would sound best with each melody of a rondo. Distribute these instruments and have the children playing them accompany the music whenever they hear their particular section.

Draw to Theme and Variations (This activity is suitable for upper elementary grades)

The children should know the meaning of "Theme." Discuss the meaning of "Variation" as compared to "change." Play a simple Theme and Variations for them. Play one variation at a time and see if the class can tell how each variation differs from the theme.

Distribute drawing paper and crayons and explain that as you play the music, they are to draw a "Theme and Variations." The theme came be a simple picture of anything at all. Every time a new variation is played, they draw, on another part of the page, the same picture again, making it a little different from the original.

A possible idea might emerge as shown in the illustration.

Other picture variations could be based on such subjects as "The Tree," "The House," "Seasons," "Flowers."

THEME: THE FACE

Label the Theme and Variations

Play the theme of a Theme and Variations several times. Have the class clap the rhythm of the melody or hum along so that they become very familiar with the theme. Prepare signs which describe each variation. If, for example, the class will listen to *Variations on Pop Goes the Weasel,* the signs could say, "SAD," "MERRY-GO-ROUND," "WALTZ," "CAN-CAN DANCE," "LAUGHTER," etc. Distribute the cards and then play the entire composition. As each variation is reached, the child holding the card which best describes that variation stands and shows it to the class.

Find the Parts That Look the Same

Distribute song books or copies of the score of a song. Have the class find the parts of the song that look the same—that have the same melody and rhythm. Then sing or play the song on the piano or song bells and have the children hear that music that looks the same will sound the same.

Create a Fugue

The class should be experienced in singing rounds and playing music imitation games such as "Follow-the-Leader," "Clap-Back," "Rhythm Instrument Echoes."

Have the pupils select a topic for the fugue. Perhaps it will be "The Weather," or "The Inflation," or "School Lunches." If, for example, the topic is "The Weather," the "subject sentence" could be, "It is raining outside! I've never seen such terrible weather!"

A fugue based on this could be developed in the following way:

1. Select four pupils as speakers and one to be the composer or conductor. Speaker One starts by saying, "It is raining outside! I've never seen such terrible weather!" Then, as Speaker One continues talking about the weather, saying anything relevant, Speaker Two says, "It is raining outside! I've never seen such terrible weather!"

2. Speaker Three enters, saying, "It is raining outside! I've never seen such terrible weather!" while Speakers One and Two continue to talk—sometimes individually, sometimes together. When Speaker Four starts with the same "subject sentence," Speakers One, Two, and Three continue to make up anything they wish to say about weather.

3. From then on, the composer or conductor will point at random to the speakers. The one to whom he or she points will immediately repeat in a loud voice, "It is raining outside! I've never seen such terrible weather!" while the other three speakers continue their part of the conversation.

4. To end the fugue, all four can say the "subject sentence" together.

Listen to a Fugue

Have the class listen to a short fugue in which the subject—or main melody—can be clearly distinguished at each repetition. Have them raise hands every time they hear the subject.

Recordings to Illustrate Musical Form:

ABA Form: Norwegian Dance, No.2, by Grieg.
Minuetto, from Divertimento No. 17 in D, by Mozart, *Adventures in Music,* Grade 5, Volume 2.
Andalucia, by Lecuona, *Adventures in Music,* Grade 4, Volume 1.
"Anitra's Dance," from *Peer Gynt* Suite, *Adventures in Music,* Grade 1, Volume 2.

Rondo: "Für Elise," by Beethoven
"Gypsy" Rondo, by Haydn
"Turkish" Rondo, by Mozart
"Dance of the Comedians," from *The Bartered Bride,* by Smetana, *Adventures in Music,* Grade 6, Volume 2.

Theme and Variations: Second Movement, *Surprise* Symphony, by Haydn.
Variations on Pop Goes the Weasel, by Caillet, *Adventures in Music,* Grade 4, Volume 1.
Variations on "Ah, Vous Dirai-Je, Maman" K.455 by Mozart (theme of "Alphabet Song").
Fourth movement, Quintet in A, ("The Trout") by Schubert.

Fugue: "Little" Fugue in G Minor, by Bach, *Adventures in Music,* Grade Six, Volume 1. (Also arrangement by Caillet on *Family Fun With Music,* RCA Victor.)
Fugue in C Minor, (Fuga Vulgaris), from *The Wurst of P.D.Q. Bach,* by Peter Schickele.

MISCELLANEOUS LISTENING
ACTIVITIES

Most of the following activities are suitable for all grade levels.

Listen to Silence

As the children remain absolutely silent for several minutes (use your judgment in deciding how long), have them listen for and mentally record every sound that they can hear. Then ask them to tell what they heard. They will have noticed things of which they were never aware—perhaps feet scraping on the floor, a door closing in the distance, paper rustling, the starting of a car engine, their neighbors' breathing. Explain to them that when we listen to music, we listen with the same attention so that we can hear as much as possible of what the composer has to express.

Have a Listening Corner

Set up a "Music Corner" in your classroom. In addition to music scrap books, music books, and stories, have a record player, some recordings, and earphones. Children who have completed an assignment will then be able, if they wish, to listen to music without disturbing the rest of the class.

The record player with earphones can also be available for emotionally disturbed or hyperactive youngsters. If they become restless, they can listen to recordings of their own choice without distracting the other children.

Make a Tape of Sounds

Make a tape of sounds in the environment—in school, in the street, at home, or in a park. Play it for your pupils and see how many of the sounds they can identify. The children can bring in sound-producing objects and they can be taped.

Write a Sound Score

Have the children write a list of sounds they can hear around them. Then have the class write a "score" indicating with line drawings or symbols what sounds were heard. (See the illustration.)

LIST OF SOUNDS HEARD

Clock ticking
Door slamming
Car going by
Footsteps
Talking
The bird, etc.

THE SCORE

Play the Sound Score

Have the children play the "sound score," using rhythm instruments, vocal sounds, and body sounds (clapping, stamping, clicking tongues) to represent the sounds. Tape the resulting "music."

Make Listening Charts

Have the children make "Listening Charts" to which they will add when they hear new music. The page is divided into a number of columns with headings such as "TITLE," "COMPOSER," "TEMPO," "METER," "TIMBRE," "DYNAMICS," "OTHER." As each new composition is heard, the pupils fill in as many of the columns as they can. If there is any doubt or disagreement about any of these aspects of the music, portions could be played again. When the appropriate answers are decided, play the music again as the class tries to hear all of these different things.

Fill in a Listening Form

Distribute work sheets. As a composition is played, have the children circle what they hear of the different aspects of the music.

The music is: Allegro, Largo, Presto.

The meter is: $\frac{2}{4}$, $\frac{3}{4}$, $\frac{4}{4}$

The music is played: *ff, pp, p*

The instrument is the: violin, clarinet, tuba

Match the Picture with the Music

Have a group of pictures displayed in front of the room (e.g., a storm at sea, a crowded city street, a peaceful night, a clown). Play a recording (e.g., the first movement of the "Moonlight" Sonata) and have the children select the picture which expresses the same mood as the music.

Be a Composer

Describe several scenes to the class and have them work out a plan for a musical composition for each scene. The plan should include their decisions about what tempo, dynamics, and musical instruments would best express the scene.

	TEMPO	DYNAMICS	INSTRUMENTS
A storm	allegro, presto	*f, ff,*	cymbals tympani whole orchestra
Birds	moderato or allegro	*p, pp* *mp, mf*	flutes piccolos
A quiet night	andante	*p, pp,* *mp*	cellos double bass clarinets viola violins
A lively party	allegro	*mf, f*	violins drums tone blocks brass instruments whole orchestra

Find the Last Note

Play any short, familiar, simple tune on the song bells—but leave out the last note. Have the children try to sing the last note and then call on volunteers to try, by playing different bars, to find that note. Do this a number of times with different songs.

Then explain that the last note is like "home base"—to finish the music, we feel as if we *must* go to that last note. This last note is also called the "key" note, so that if the music ends on C, it is the key ("home") of C; if it ends on G, it is in the key ("home") of G, and so on.

Compose Twelve-Tone Music

In Western music, there are twelve tones within the range of an octave. An octave means eight notes apart, e.g., the tone C to any C above or below it; the tone A to any A above or below it, and so on. The keyboard in the illustration shows the twelve tones.

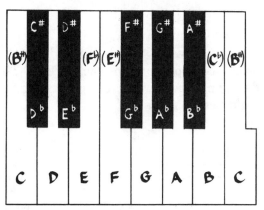

♯—sharp; ½ step (the next note on the
    keyboard up from a given note)

♭—flat; ½ step down from a given note

Have the class name the twelve tones in any order at all, never repeating any of them. They will have composed a twelve-tone melody.

C, A♯, G, F♯, B, D, G♯, E, A, F, D♯, C♯

Then write the same tones backwards:

C♯, D♯, F, A, E, G♯, D, B, F♯, G, A♯, C

Have a volunteer play the melodies on song bells. You can also distribute the twelve tones from the resonator bells to twelve children and have them play the melodies, each one hitting his or her bell in turn. Point out that twelve-tone melodies are a type of modern, twentieth century music.

Listen to Twelve-Tone Music

After a few experiences of this type, play a brief twelve-tone composition for the children so that they can hear how this type of music sounds, (e.g., Serenade, Opus 24, by Schönberg).

Listen to Minor Music

Play a very simple three-note tune on the song bells, using the bars G, A, and B. Then play the same thing again, this time changing all the B's to B flats (the symbol for flat is ♭). The B flat is found on the black bar just below the B.

Hot Cross Buns	Change to
B, A, G	B♭, A, G
B, A, G	B♭, A, G
G, G, G, G	G, G, G, G
A, A, A, A	A, A, A, A,
B, A, G	B♭, A, G

Merrily We Roll Along	Changed
B, A, G, A, B, B, B	B♭, A, G, A, B♭, B♭, B♭
A, A, A	A, A, A
B, B, B	B♭, B♭, B♭
B, A, G, A, B, B, B	B♭, A, G, A, B♭, B♭, B♭
A, A, B, A, G	A, A, B♭, A, G

Do the same thing for a five-note melody (g, a, b, c, d) such as "Go Tell Aunt Rhodie."

Go Tell Aunt Rhodie	Changed
B, B, A, G, G	B♭, B♭, A, G, G
A, A, C, B, A, G	A, A, C, B♭, A, G
D, D, C, B, B	D, D, C, B♭, B♭
A, G, A, B, G	A, G, A, B♭, G

Explain that the quality of sound when you play B is called "major"; when you play B flat, it is called "minor."

Have the children try to describe the differences in mood and effect between major and minor.

Decide Whether the Music Is Major or Minor

Play a recording, or sing, or, if you can, play on the piano or song bells a series of brief melodies and have the children indicate on work sheets which tunes are "major" and which are "minor." (If identifying major and minor is a new experience for you, you could ask a friend with a good music background to help you decide which melodies are major and which are minor. After a while, the difference will seem obvious to you.)

An example of a work sheet is shown in the illustration.

Finish the pictures to show whether the songs are major or minor:

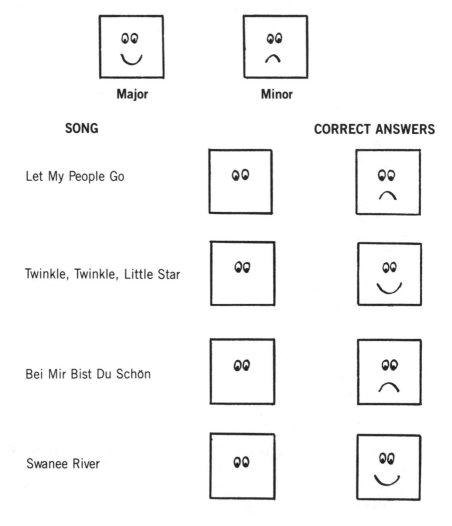

Find the Differences in the Music (Team Game)

Divide the class into two teams. Play two contrasting compositions without telling the children what the titles are. Have them list all the differences they can find. See which team can find more differences.

A Music	B Music
f	p
minor	major
allegro	andante
melody high pitched	melody low pitched
trumpet playing	cello playing

Specific Activities for Specific Compositions

Most of the following compositions are classified as "program music"—music with extramusical associations, either describing a scene or person or telling a story. Only *some* music is program music and it is *not* at all necessary to know the program in order to enjoy the music. If the music has a story which you'd like the class to know, by all means, tell it to them.

Don't, however, make up your own story for music which has none and then tell the children that this is what the music is about. Where music has no program indicated by the composer, anyone's interpretation is valid and another person's should not be imposed.

If you ask your pupils to make up their own stories for the music, encourage them to use their imaginations and to express their feelings. Anything they create is fine. It is not fair to ask them what *they* think the music is about and then reject any part of what they say, or to tell them, "No, it's *really* about..."

Carnival of the Animals, by Saint-Saëns

Display large pictures of several of the animals described in Saint-Saëns' *Carnival of the Animals* (e.g., lion, fish, swan, elephant, turtle). Play one of the sections and have the children decide which of the animals is being described. Have them give the reasons for their decision.

Adventures of a Zoo, by Kleinsinger

This work has a narration introducing the animals—lion, mouse, elephant, giraffe, kangaroo, monkey. Play the Introduction for the class and then select volunteers to represent each of the animals. As the music is played again, the child representing a particular animal pantomimes its movements.

Overture to *William Tell,* by Rossini

Tell the class the story of William Tell—his country's struggle for freedom, his being required to shoot an apple off his son's head, the final victory over tyranny. Inform them that the music they will hear will describe the moods of the story—peaceful scenes, the coming struggle (or storm), the struggle and final triumph (known to all as the "Lone Ranger" music.) As the music is played, have them draw any of the scenes from the story.

"Russian Dance" and "Arabian Dance" from *The Nutcracker Suite* by Tchaikowsky

Student volunteers can make up suitable dances for these selections. The class can also draw to the music, designing stage sets or costumes for these portions of the ballet.

"March" from *The Nutcracker Suite,* by Tchaikowsky

Have the children listen to the music, noting where the cymbal crashes occur. Replay the piece, this time having them pretend to play the cymbals at the exact moment the instrument is heard in the music. Two children at a time can take turns playing the cymbals along with the orchestra.

(This activity is excellent for developing careful listening, control, and familiarity with the composition.)

The Sorcerer's Apprentice, by Dukas

Prepare transparencies illustrating different parts of the story. Tell the story of the music and then, as the recording is played, project the transparencies at the appropriate times. (This same activity can be done with any story in music.)

Danse Macabre, by Saint-Saëns

Prepare signs describing the music: "THE CLOCK STRIKES TWELVE"; "DEATH TUNES HIS VIOLIN"; "SKELETONS JOIN THE DANCE"; "THE MUSIC GETS FASTER AND FASTER"; "THE DANCE GETS WILDER AND WILDER"; "SUDDENLY, THE CLOCK CROWS"; "IT IS MORNING"; "THE DANCE MUSIC STOPS"; "THE GHOSTS AND GOBLINS DISAPPEAR"; "ALL IS QUIET AGAIN."

Tell the class what the music will represent and distribute the signs. As each part of the music is reached, the child holding the appropriate sign stands and shows it to the class.

"Baba Yaga" ("The Little Hut on Chicken Legs") from *Pictures at an Exhibition,* by Moussorgsky

Baba Yaga is a Russian fairy-tale figure—a witch who is so ugly that she hides inside a little hut that runs around on chicken legs, coming out only on the Russian equivalent of our Halloween. Play the music for the class. Then, as they hear it again, have them draw their versions of what Baba Yaga or her house might look like.

"Gnomus," from *Pictures at an Exhibition,* by Moussorgsky

Ask the children to imagine, as they listen to the music, what or who is moving. Have volunteers show how they think the "THING" is moving.

"Circus Music," from *The Red Pony,* by Copland

This music, about a circus, describes many of the performers. Play the recording for the children and let them decide who is represented by each melody. Play the recording again, having volunteers act out or dance the roles of the circus performers. This could develop into an interesting "ballet." Some of the children can design costumes or sets.

A POSTSCRIPT ABOUT LISTENING ACTIVITIES

There are many ways in which children can be actively involved while learning about what they can listen for in music—pantomiming, dancing, clapping, moving, playing rhythm instruments, dramatizing, story telling, drawing pictures, using visual aids, singing, theme counting, creating music, classifying, analyzing, chanting, cutting out and pasting pictures, paper and pencil work, and recording sounds.

The fact, however, that these activities *can* be used does not mean that they *must* always be used; it is important and enjoyable to just sit and listen to music. With the development of understanding and the proper choice of music, this can become one of the most valuable and loved activities in music.

6

Fun with
Classroom
Instruments

THE AUTOHARP

The autoharp (automatic harp) is a delightful instrument. Played by simultaneously strumming the strings and pressing a button indicating the name of the desired chord, it provides background harmonies. (See the illustration.)

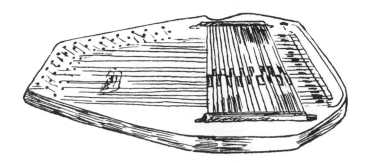

The same chord indications are used for guitar and autoharp.

When the bar labeled C is pressed and the autoharp is strummed, the C major chord (tones C,E,G) will be heard. Press the G bar and the sounded chord will be G major (the tones G,B,D). Little or no practice is needed to play the autoharp.

If there is no musician, music teacher, or someone experienced in tuning guitars or autoharps to help you, you can tune the instrument by following the instructions and using the tuning tool that comes with the autoharp. Use a set of song bells to help you hear the pitch for each string.

Play the Autoharp Using One Chord

Give the children a chance to accompany singing. A number of songs can be accompanied using only one chord (or bar of the autoharp). One child can play the accompaniment, or two can share the work—one child pressing the indicated bar while the second child strums on the strong beat.

The following songs can be harmonized with just one chord.

LIZA JANE

Verse 2: Got a house in Baltimore,
        Li'l Liza Jane,
        Lots of children 'round the door,
        Li'l Liza Jane.

THERE'S A HOLE IN THE BUCKET

(The boys sing Georgie's part; the girls sing Liza's.) AMERICAN FOLK SONG

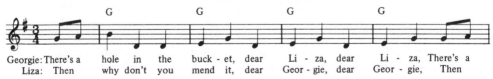

G	G	G	G

hole   in   the   buck - et,   dear   Li - za,   a_____   hole!
why   don't   you   mend   it,   dear   Geor - gie,   mend the   hole!

Verse 2: Georgie: With what should I mend it dear Liza, dear Liza,
                          With what should I mend it, dear Liza, with what?
         Liza: With a straw you should mend it, dear Georgie, dear Georgie,
                          With a straw you should mend it, dear Georgie, with a straw.

Verse 3: Georgie: But the straw is too long, dear Liza, dear Liza....
         Liza: Then why don't you cut it, dear Georgie, dear Georgie....

Verse 4: Georgie: With what should I cut it, dear Liza....
         Liza: With a knife, you should cut it, dear Georgie....

Verse 5: Georgie: But the knife is too dull....
         Liza: Then why don't you hone it....

Verse 6: Georgie: With what should I hone it....
         Liza: With a stone you should hone it....

Verse 7: Georgie: But the stone is too dry....
         Liza: Then why don't you wet it....

Verse 8: Georgie: With what should I wet it....
         Liza: With water you wet it....

Verse 9: Georgie: With what should I fetch it....
         Liza: With a bucket you fetch it....

Verse 10: Georgie: But there's a hole in the bucket, dear Liza....

MY GOOSE

OLD ENGLISH ROUND

Why should - n't my goose, Sing as well as thy goose,

When I payed for my goose, Twice as much as thou?

FOR HEALTH AND STRENGTH

ENGLISH ROUND

For health and strength and dai - ly food we give our thanks each day.

FRÈRE JACQUES

FRENCH ROUND

Frè - re Jac - ques, Frè - re Jac - ques, Dor - mez vous? Dor - mez vous?

Son-nez les ma - ti - nes, Son-nez les ma - ti - nes, Ding - dong-dong. Ding - dong-dong.

English: Are you sleeping, are you sleeping,
        Brother John, Brother John,
        Morning bells are ringing,
        Morning bells are ringing,
        Ding, dong dong;
        Ding dong, dong.

LITTLE TOMMY TINKER

ROUND; TRADITIONAL

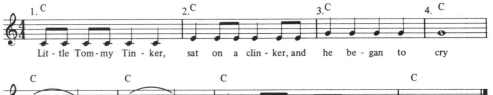

Lit - tle Tom - my Tin - ker, sat on a clin - ker, and he be - gan to cry

Ma,_____ Ma,_____ poor lit - tle in - no - cent guy.

LITTLE DAVID

NEGRO SPIRITUAL

Refrain:

Lit - tle Da - vid, play on your harp, Hal - le - lu, Ha - le - lu! Lit-tle Da - vid,

play on your harp, Ha - le - lu! lu! 1. Lit - tle Da - vid, was a

shep - herd boy He killed Go - li - ath and shout - ed for joy.

Verse 2: Joshua was the son of Nun,
He never would quit
'til his work was done.

Verse 3: I told you once, I told you twice,
You can't get to heaven by
shooting dice.

SWING LOW, SWEET CHARIOT

NEGRO SPIRITUAL

Verse 2: If you get there before I do,
Coming for to carry me home,
Just tell my friends I'm coming too,
Coming for to carry me home.

SHALOM CHAVERIM

ISRAELI SONG

Shalom: A Hebrew greeting; it can mean
          hello, farewell, or peace be with
          you.
Chaverim: friends
Le-hit-ra-ot: See you again; farewell,
              so long.

English words:
    Peace to you, friends,
    Oh, peace to you friends,
    Shalom! Shalom!
    We'll meet once again, we'll meet once again,
    Shalom! Shalom!

Play the Autoharp Using Two Chords

Two-chord accompaniments are also simple and can supply the harmonies for many, many (literally, hundreds) songs. As before, let one child play the accompaniment, following the chord indications in the music, or divide the playing between two children.

Among the songs needing just two chords are:

Down in the Valley	Long, Long Ago
Lightly Row	Billy Boy*
This Old Man, He Played One*	Merrily We Roll Along
Go Tell Aunt Rhodie	Tom Dooley
Oh, My Darling Clementine	Yellow Rose of Texas
Skip to My Lou	Where Has My Little Dog Gone?
Shoo Fly, Don't Bother Me	Cockles and Mussels
Hail, Hail, The Gang's All Here	He's Got the Whole World in His Hands
Did You Ever See a Lassie?	Cindy
Hush, Little Baby	Joshua Fit the Battle of Jericho
Polly Wolly Doodle	The Bowery
Santa Lucia	
Blow the Man Down	

---

*Scores for these songs are provided in Chapter 7, in the section on using music to teach arithmetic concepts.

Except for "Joshua Fit the Battle of Jericho" which is harmonized with d minor and A7 chords, all the other songs on the list can be accompanied by one of the following combinations of chords:

C; G7

F; C7

G; D7

Play the Autoharp Using Color Coding

Some children may find it difficult to locate the specific bars for chords indicated in the music. In those cases, playing the autoharp can be made very simple through the use of color coding. If, for example, the three chords G, C, D7 are needed, circle all the G chord indications in the music with red crayon, the C's with yellow, and the D7's with green. Then, using a washable marker, color the light portion of the G, C, and D_7 bars with the matching colors.

The child sees the color in the music score and pushes the button of the same color on the autoharp.

Accompany Songs with Autoharp

Chord indications for the autoharp frequently appear in the music score. Because you can sit facing the children and close to them while you play the autoharp, it is an excellent instrument for accompaniments. Try to use it often.

PLAYING BOTTLES

Make Tuned Bottles or Jars; Play Three-Note Melodies

Using three jars or bottles of similar size and shape, add different amounts of water to each so that when they are tapped gently with a spoon, musical tones will result. Adjust the amount of water in each so that the first three tones of a scale (e.g., F, G, A; C, D, E; or G, A, B) can be played. (Check with the song bells to get the right pitch.) Let the children take turns making up their own tunes on the bottles or playing three-note songs like "Hot Cross Buns" or "Mary Had a Little Lamb."

Play Five-Note Songs on Tuned Jars or Bottles

Tune five jars or bottles by adding or subtracting water so that you can play the first five tones of a scale (e.g., C,D,E,F,G;

G,A,B,C,D). Let the children experiment with the bottles, creating their own tunes. Suggest to them that anything they play will be fine. If the notes C,D,E,F,G are used, they might want to play C as the last tone. If G,A,B,C,D are used, G could be the "home" or key tone.

SONG BELLS

Create Pentatonic Melodies Using Song Bells

Perhaps the most important contribution of the Orff Method is the use of the pentatonic scale—not only to develop creativity but in learning specially composed and arranged music. Special instruments of the highest quality are used.

Play a rhythmic pattern on the black bars of the song bells in any order at all. A melody will result.

You are using the tones of the pentatonic (five-tone) scale. Notice that on any keyboard, the patterns of two black and three black note groups keep repeating. Each group of five black keys makes up a pentatonic scale.

For some reason, the music of many peoples, including American Indian, Japanese, Chinese, Scottish, Afro-American, Hungarian, and African, as well as many American folk and popular tunes, are frequently based on tunes which can be played on the black keys of a piano.

Give the children many opportunities to improvise pentatonic melodies. This is a fine activity for retarded children because the results are so immediately satisfying.

Play Questions and Answers on the Song Bells

Use two sets of song bells. Mark the F ♯ (F ♯ is the first black note immediately above F) with white chalk. Distribute the bells to two children. The first child creates a pentatonic melody using the black bars and ending on any bar except the F ♯. The second child plays an "answer" based on the pentatonic scale, ending on F ♯.

Encourage the children to extend their questions and answers. The results will be almost uniformly delightful.

Play Pentatonic Duets

Use two sets of melody bells. Have one child play an *ostinato* (an "obstinate" or "stubborn" melody) by repeating a small rhythmic fragment of melody again and again. As the ostinato is played on one set of bells, a second child improvises a pentatonic melody on the other song bells.

Play Pentatonic Trios

Use three sets of melody bells. One child plays a pentatonic ostinato. The other two children play pentatonic "questions" and "answers."

Two children can make up pentatonic ostinato parts and play them on the song bells while a third child creates a pentatonic melody.

Play an Indian Song

Have a child set a steady beat on the tom-tom as another plays the notes D ♯ and A ♯ on a piano or with two mallets on the song bells.

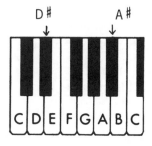

At the same time, a third child improvises a pentatonic (black key) melody on the piano or another set of song bells, ending on the tone D ♯. The resulting effect will simulate an Indian dance or song.

RESONATOR BELLS

Use Resonator Bells

The resonator bells are similar in appearance to song bells except that each bar is attached to a resonator in the form of a hollow block of wood. (See the illustration.)

In addition, all of the bells can be separated from the set and as many as desired distributed to the children. Thus, melodies can be played by one child, or a group of children can participate, each one playing one or more bells. The tones of the resonator bells are sweet, delicate, and chime-like.

Improvise Melodies on Resonator Bells

Remove the black bars from the resonator bell set and place them on a table. Have the children take turns improvising pentatonic melodies.

Improvise Pentatonic Questions and Answers
Using Resonator Bells and Song Bells

Use one set of song bells and one set of resonator bells. Have two children improvise pentatonic "questions" and "answers" —one child creating a melody on the song bells and the second child "answering" using the resonator bells. Then, reverse, having the "question" on the resonator bells and the "answer" (ending on F ♯) on the song bells.

Have a Classroom Orchestra

Select one child as conductor. Use three sets of song bells, a set of resonator bells, and any combination of rhythm instruments selected by the children (e.g., drum, tambourine, jingle bells). The conductor sets the beat. The drum starts to play rhythmic patterns. One child plays an ostinato on the song bells. The child at the resonator bells plays on the black bars, a mallet in each hand. He or she hits any two of the black notes simultaneously in any random order. The important thing is to keep the rhythm.

Two children play "questions" and "answers" improvisations on the other two sets of melody bells. The other percussion instruments join the ensemble. The conductor can indicate when the different rhythm instruments should play or they can improvise their own accompaniments.

Play Duets with Autoharp and Resonator Bells

Distribute resonator bells as follows:

Child One: C, E, G

Child Two: G, B, D, F

Give one child the autoharp and have him strum either the C chord or G7 chord, according to patterns written on the board. When the C chord is played, Child One plays his or her resonator bells in any order to create a melody. When the G7 chord is sounded, Child Two plays a melody on his or her resonator bells. The last tone of the melodies played by Child One should be C. Possible patterns could be:

1. Autoharp plays:
   Resonator Bells:

C	G7	G7	C
Child One plays	Child Two plays	Child 2	Child 1

2. Autoharp:
   Resonator Bells:

G7	C	G7	C
Child 2	Child 1	Child 2	Child 1

3. Autoharp:
   Resonator Bells:

C	C	G7	C
Child 1	Child 1	Child 2	Child 1

4. Autoharp:
   Resonator Bells:

G7	G7	G7	C
Child 2	Child 2	Child 2	Child 2

Accompany Songs with Bells

Check to see if the autoharp chord indications of a song include only those from the following list and distribute those Swiss Melody Bells (hand-held) or resonator bells which are needed to form the indicated chords:

The Chord	Bells Needed
F	F, A, C
B♭	B♭, D, F
C7	C, E, G, B♭
g minor	G, B♭, D

List the above tone combinations on the chalkboard and point to them according to the chord indications in the score. As the class sings the song, the children holding the bells accompany the song by playing the particular combinations of tones which would provide the harmonies. (This activity can be extended to include the autoharp playing the accompaniment together with the bells.)

ADDITIONAL ACTIVITIES USING RHYTHM INSTRUMENTS

A number of activities incorporating rhythm instruments have been described in previous chapters. These have included reading rhythmic notation, improvising, accompanying movement activities and recordings. These activities have been used to aid in developing the sense of pitch (through use of song bells and hand-held bells) and the sense of rhythm, and in learning concepts of tempo, rhythm, notation, dynamics, and musical form.

There are other creative and enjoyable ways to use rhythm instruments to reinforce music concepts and to have pleasurable experiences with music.

The rhythm band is not only for primary grades. Fifth and sixth graders (and seventh and eighth) are just as eager to play bongos, snare drums, maracas, cymbals, and other percussion instruments. Through experiences with rhythm instruments, they can derive great joy—releasing tensions, discovering sounds, developing an understanding of new concepts and gaining skills in creating music.

Explore the Rhythm Instruments

Introduce one instrument at a time. Let the pupils take turns playing the instrument and experimenting with it to discover how many different ways one can play it and how many different kinds of sounds it can make.

The tambourine, for example, can be struck with the flat or open hand, or fist, or knuckles. It can be shaken, tapped with the fingers, struck against the head, elbow, shoulder, hip, or knee. It can be played with a mallet or a pencil, or the metal discs can be whirled with the fingers. See how creative your class can be with this and other instruments.

Find the Rhythm Instruments

After young children have become somewhat familiar with the rhythm instruments, place some on a table. Then sing about one instrument at a time:

Where is the drum___

Call on a volunteer to come to the front of the room, find the instrument and play it, singing:

Here it___ is___

Take Your Turn

Distribute five or six different instruments and start to play a composition (a recording or at the piano). Call out the name of an instrument and the child holding that instrument starts to play with the music. When you name another instrument, the first child stops playing and the child holding the second named instrument starts to play. Continue until all have had turns at playing.

Play Instrument "Musical Chairs"

Distribute rhythm instruments and have the children play them to the rhythm of a recording. When the music is stopped, the children stop playing. Repeat this a number of times, varying the length of time the children play before you stop the record. This activity will make them aware of stops in the music; it will sharpen their listening ability, and help them to develop impulse control.

Have a Parade

Play a recording of a stirring march and let the children have a parade. Have several of them accompany the music with drums, rhythm sticks, and cymbals. If there are any physically disabled children in the class, they can participate in the parade by playing the accompaniment, or, if they are in wheel chairs, by having their chairs moved by other children—their "music partners."

Have a Country Western Band

Use spoons struck together, a washboard scraped with a stick, a few kazoos, and some rhythm sticks to accompany American folk-song games and dances (e.g., "Cindy," "Arkansas Traveller," "Comin' Round the Mountain," "Jimmy Crack Corn.")

Play Three Different Rhythms

Distribute two or three each of three types of instruments (e.g., drums, maracas, rhythm sticks). Select a song and tell the children to keep that song in mind as they play. The first group plays a steady beat on the first count of each measure. The second group plays a steady beat on every count, and the third group plays the rhythm of the melody.

YANKEE DOODLE

Create an Arch Form Composition

Give different rhythm instruments to each of four or five children and select a volunteer to be the conductor. Have each child create a rhythmic pattern for his or her instrument and then instruct them to start playing in a set order and then stop in reverse order. The conductor will signal each child when it is his or her turn to start and when to stop playing.

Instruments playing

Maracas play.
Maracas and bells play.
Maracas, bells, and drum play.
Maracas, bells, drum, and tambourine play.
Maracas, bells, and drum play.
Maracas and bells play.
Maracas play.

Diagram the resulting music and draw a curved line showing its musical form which can be compared to the shape of an arch:

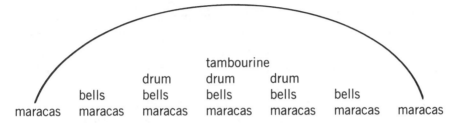

Create a Rhythm Rondo

Tell the class that they will create a rhythm rondo (always coming around again to the main theme). Distribute rhythm instruments to several children and have one of them play the main theme—any rhythmic pattern he or she can create. Point alternately to any one or more of the other players and then to the main theme player again. Continue this until there are four or five returns of the main theme. The result will be a rhythm rondo.

Let other children take turns playing the main theme and the other instruments. One of the children can be the conductor to signal the players when to start and stop playing.

Create Rhythm ABA Form

Distribute rhythm instruments to two groups of children. One group plays the A section, creating their own rhythms. The second group, representing a different combination of instruments, plays the B section, and then the A group repeats its part.

This can be combined with movement, having different children choreograph for the A and the B sections. The A and B sections should have strong contrasts, not only in movement and the choice of instruments used, but in dynamics, rhythm patterns, and tempo.

Accompany Songs with Rhythm Band Instruments

The performance of many songs can be enhanced by rhythm band instruments. Latin American songs can be accompanied by bongos, claves, maracas, castanets, and tambourines. Finger cymbals and tone blocks are appropriate for songs of Oriental origin. Cowboy melodies can have rhythm sticks and tone blocks in the background to imitate horses cantering or trotting while American Indian songs call for the tom-tom and snare drums and cymbals are "naturals" for marching songs.

Guide the children in deciding which instruments would be most appropriate and which rhythmic patterns they should play. Dynamics, form, tempo, type and mood of the song, tone quality and method of playing (banging or shaking) the instruments should all be considered. Limit the number of instruments distributed to avoid having the accompaniment drown out the singers.

Some songs that are especially suitable for or specifically call for rhythm band accompaniments follow.

HICKORY DICKORY DOCK

To represent the ticking of a clock, have the rhythm sticks and tone blocks beat a steady rhythm:

On the word, "One," the cymbals crash; on the word "down," the triangle is struck.

This song can be dramatized.

(Note: ⌒ = fermata; pause; hold for extra time.)

I'M A FINE MUSICIAN

GERMAN

Each time the song is repeated, call out, in random order, the name of one of the instruments. The child holding that instrument plays the refrain in time to the music, while the other children sing.

Drum: Boom and boom and boom and boom; boom and boom and boom and boom.

Rhythm Sticks: Click and click and click and click...

Triangle: Tinkle, tinkle, tinkle, tink...

Maracas: Shake and shake and shake and shake...

Cymbals: Crash and crash and crash and crash...

LA RASPA

MEXICAN

keep   a   stead - y   beat,   What   does   the   mu - sic   say?   La - la

la - la - la...

Part A: Use "banging" instruments—rhythm sticks, drum, tone blocks—played in time to the steady beat of the music.

Part B: Use "shaking" instruments—maracas and tambourines.

JINGLE BELLS

TRADITIONAL

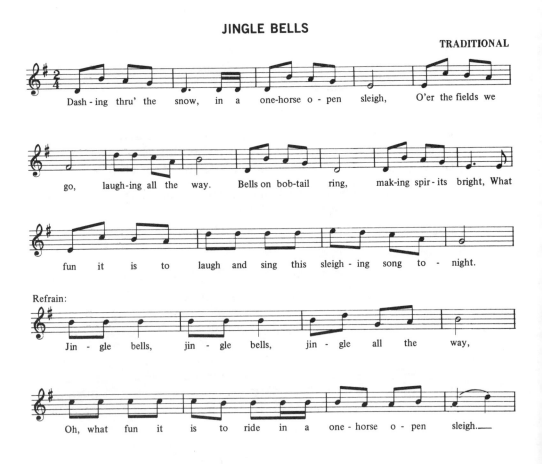

Dash - ing thru' the   snow,   in a   one-horse o - pen   sleigh,   O'er the fields we

go,   laugh-ing all the   way.   Bells on bob-tail   ring,   mak-ing spir - its bright, What

fun   it   is   to   laugh and   sing   this   sleigh - ing   song   to - night.

Refrain:

Jin - gle   bells,   jin - gle   bells,   jin - gle   all   the   way,

Oh,   what   fun   it   is   to   ride   in   a   one - horse o - pen   sleigh.___

Jin - gle bells, jin - gle bells, jin - gle all the way,

Oh, what fun it is to ride in a one - horse o - pen sleigh.

Use tone blocks and rhythm sticks in a steady rhythm throughout to represent horse trotting. Add sleigh bells at the refrain. At the very end, have one stroke on the tambourine as indicated in the music.

GET ON BOARD

NEGRO SPIRITUAL

Get on board, lit - tle chil - dren, Get on board, lit - tle chil-dren, Get on

board, lit - tle chil - dren, there's room for man - y a more. The

gos - pel train's a - com - ing, I hear it just at hand,___ I

hear the car wheels rum - bling and roll - ing thru' the land.

Use rhythm instruments to simulate the sound of a train:

Maracas and sticks (click-clack of wheels):

Sandpaper blocks (chug-chug of engine):
Add whistle and/or bells.

SONG OF THE DESERT
(CARAVAN)

F.B.   Adapted from an Arab Chant

Slowly

1. Car - a - van   slow - ly ap-pear - ing,   Car - a - van   on   the ho - ri - zon,
2. Car - a - van   heav - y with jew - els,   Car - a - van   trin - kets and spic - es,

Cam - els sway - ing   in the des-ert heat,   Tin - kling bells and   pad-ding on their feet,
Car - pets, lac - es, feath-ers for a queen, Rar - est trea - sures ev - er   to be seen,

Slow   -   ly   mov - ing in the night,   Slow   -   ly   com - ing in - to sight
Slow   -   ly   drift - ing in the night, Slow   -   ly   drift-ing out of sight.

Lower Voices

Car - a - van,   car - a - van,

Introduction (add one instrument at a time until all are playing):

Drum: Camels' swaying

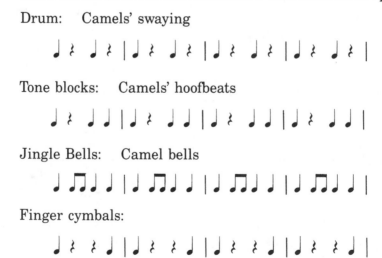

Tone blocks: Camels' hoofbeats

Jingle Bells: Camel bells

Finger cymbals:

Start the song when all the instruments are playing. After both verses are done, gradually drop out instruments in reverse order until the caravan disappears and all is silent. The music should start softly and gradually become louder and louder as the caravan approaches and passes. Then there should be a gradual decrescendo as the caravan goes farther and farther away.

OVER THE RIVER AND THROUGH THE WOODS

Words by **LYDIA MARIA CHILD**
Composer unkown

Use jingle bells to represent sleigh bells and tone blocks to represent horse cantering. Keep a steady rhythm throughout:

Create a Rhythm Band Accompaniment for Orchestral Compositions

Have the children listen carefully to a recording of a short orchestral composition to decide which rhythm instruments could be used as an accompaniment. Musical form, tempo, mood, dynamics, the method of playing the instruments, and tone quality should all be considered, but there is no one "correct" way. Musical feelings can be expressed in many ways.

Distribute the instruments selected by the children and replay the recording as those having the instruments accompany the music.

Accompany Songs with a Classroom Music Ensemble

Select a song for which the autoharp chords are indicated in the score. Develop a rhythm band accompaniment with the children. Distribute the autoharp, the selected rhythm instruments, and those resonator bells which comprise the tones of the chord indications. All these instruments can play together to provide accompaniments for songs.

Simple harmonies can be provided by the following chords:

The Chord	The Tones in the Chord
C	C,E,G
D7	D, F♯, A, C
F	F, A, C
G	G, B, D
G7	G, B, D, F
g minor	G, B♭, D
a minor	A, C, E
C7	C, E, G, B♭
B♭	B♭, D, F

Introduce Rhythm Band Score Reading

If you wish to have your class play a set rhythm band accompaniment—one which they have developed—the concept of score reading can gradually be developed. As a first step, you can use symbolic drawings of the instruments to indicate when each one should be played. (See the illustration.)

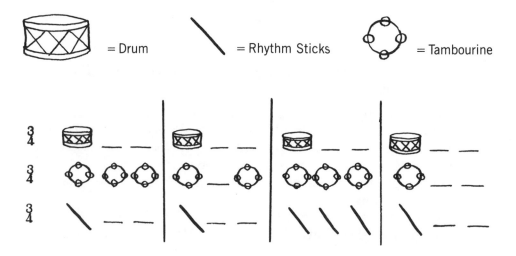

Later, when the children are familiar with simple rhythmic notation, the "picture score" can be changed to:

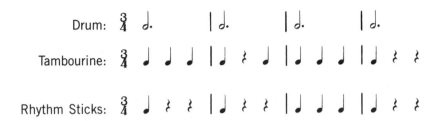

Make Rhythm Band Instruments

No rhythm band instruments? Do the Kindergarten and first grade classes have all of them in the school? This should be no problem at all. Have the children make and decorate their own instruments. This could be an excellent crafts project.

Drums

Use empty cereal boxes, large containers from canned food, hat boxes, potato chip cans. Remove the cover or lid from one or two ends. Tightly stretch over the receptacle part of the inner tube of a tire or a heavy balloon, a piece of vinyl or rubberized crib sheet—any resilient, elasticized material. You can use cord or heavy boot laces to hold it in place. A really fine "kettle drum" can be made from a metal scrub bucket and a crib sheet.

Maracas

Use any solid container (metal or cardboard) of suitable size and put into it pebbles, macaroni, rice, dried peas or beans. Hold it in two hands and shake, or insert a plastic fork or spoon, pencil, or short wooden stick as a handle. Some fine maracas can be made from bouncing balls or papier maché.

Tambourines

These can be made from aluminum pie tins or paper plates with flattened bottle caps attached.

Sandpaper Blocks

These are easy to make; use sandpaper glued or tacked onto toy building blocks.

Jingle Bells

Buy these (especially around Christmas time) at variety stores and attach them to ribbons or to the rims of paper plates.

Tone Blocks and/or Rhythm Sticks

Use two rulers struck together or pencils tapping on desks; or, look for smooth sticks (cut-down broom handles would be fine) of approximately the right size.

Through the use of your own and the children's imagination and creativity, you can make many fine percussion instruments suitable for classroom use.

MAINSTREAMING AND CLASSROOM INSTRUMENTS

All children, regardless of handicap, can participate in playing classroom instruments.

Physically handicapped children who may be unable to use one arm can share the playing of a rhythm instrument with another child; one child can hold the instrument, the other one can strike it with a mallet. You may find that hyperactive or emotionally disturbed children will be helped in developing self-esteem by becoming the "rhythm partner" of such a handicapped youngster.

Children who are hard of hearing can observe and imitate movements while playing the different instruments. In this way, they can develop and express their feeling for rhythm.

Mentally retarded children can, in addition to using color coding, play a part in classroom performances. When autoharp accompaniments become more complex, they can sing the songs. Conversely, when the song becomes too involved for them, they can play a simple beat for rhythm accompaniments.

Thus, with some playing a steady beat, some singing, some reading complex rhythmic or melodic notation, one or two playing autoharp and some playing melody or resonator bells, all of the children can be working together at their own intellectual level to perform and to create music.

7

Music in the Classroom Curriculum

Try this. Read these syllables to a highly intelligent adult and see if he can repeat them: "fa, see, kay, ef, es, yut, see, zee, bat, ex, mum, be, gee, la, hah, ray, ne, pew, dee ..." Chances are, he will have difficulty. Yet, little preschoolers can learn to say an alphabet that makes no more sense to them than these nonsense syllables would make to an adult. That is because they can say the sounds rhythmically.

Because it adds pleasure to learning and increases motivation and interest, music can enhance learning in many areas of the curriculum and at all grade levels. It can become a highly valuable integral part of the teaching-learning process.

LANGUAGE ARTS

Be the Alphabet (for Early Childhood classes)

To the tune of "Hokey Pokey," have the children assume the shapes of the letters of the alphabet as best they can with body position and arms. (See the illustration.)

They then sing:

> I make myself a C,
> I make myself a C,
> I give myself a shake, shake, shake,
> And turn myself around.

Rhythmic body positioning becomes another experience for helping children to remember some of the letters.

Sing a B Song

Have the children sing "My Bonnie Lies Over the Ocean." Every time they come to a word starting with "B," they raise hands:

> My Bonnie lies over the ocean,
> My Bonnie lies over the sea,
> My Bonnie lies over the ocean,
> Oh, bring back my Bonnie to me.
> Bring back, bring back,
> Oh, bring back my Bonnie to me, to me ...

An exciting variation of this game can be played by having the class start to sing while seated. Every time they come to a word starting with "B" they change position. If seated, they stand. If standing, they sit.

Sing a Grammar Song About "Is" and "Are" (Early Childhood)

Have a series of cards on each of which is drawn one or more objects—cats, circles, stars, faces. Hold up the cards in random order. If there is one item on the card, the children sing, to the tune of "Frère Jacques":

> There is one face, there is one face,
> There it is, there it is,
> There is only one face, there is only one face,
> There it is. There it is.

If more than one item appears, the children sing:

> There are some stars, there are some stars,
> There they are, there they are,
> There are some stars, there are some stars,
> There they are, there they are.

Find Two of the Same (Pre-Reading Skills)

Have charts prepared showing rows of objects. In each row, make two of the items the same; the rest, different. (See the illustration.)

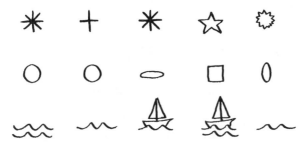

As the children sing to the tune of "London Bridge Is Falling Down," they take turns coming to the chart and circling the two items of a row that are the same:

> Two of these are just the same,
> Just the same, just the same,
> Two of these are just the same,
> My fair lady.

Find the Same Letters

Prepare charts showing rows of letters of the alphabet. In each row, two of the letters should be the same. As in the previous game, the children take turns finding and circling those in each row which are the same, singing as they do: "Two of these are just the same … my fair lady."

> If you find them, say the name,
> Say the name, say the name,
> If you find them, say the name,
> My fair lady.

It takes time and effort to make these charts. To conserve them for future use, you can cover them with clear plastic adhesive paper and have the children circle the items with washable crayons.

Use Songs to Reinforce Sight Words

Songs that have frequent repetitions of a specific word can be used to help reinforce sight reading of the word. For example, take the word, "happy."

Write on the chalkboard several sentences that contain the word "happy."

Jim was happy to go.

The boy was happy.

The happy girl had a dog.

Have the children sing to the song "If You're Happy," emphasizing the word "happy":

If you're *happy* and you know it, find the word,

If you're *happy* and you know it, find the word,

If you're *happy* and you know it,

Then your face will surely show it,

If you're *happy* and you know it, find the word.

As they sing, one of the children comes to the board and circles the word "happy" wherever it can be found.

Other possible sight words in songs can be:

"Farm," in "Old McDonald Had a Farm"

"Man," in "This Old Man"

Use Word Chants to Learn Long and Short Vowels

Place on the chalkboard the symbols for long and short vowels (e.g., ă, ā; ĭ, ī; ĕ, ē). Have the children chant as they write in the air the appropriate symbol for long or short vowels:

ă is short!

ă is short!

Short, short, short,

ă is short!

ā is long, ⎯⎯⎯

ā is long, ⎯⎯⎯

Long, ⎯⎯⎯ Long, ⎯⎯⎯

ā is long ⎯⎯⎯.

ĭ is short, etc.

Sing a Song About Long and Short Vowels

Put on the chalkboard the long and short vowels being studied. Make up lists of words with short and long vowels similar to the following:

ă	ā
măn	māne
căn	cāne
măt	māte
hăt	hāte
păn	pāne
văn	vāne

As you point to the symbols and the words, have the children sing to the tune of "Twinkle, Twinkle, Little Star":

ă is short and ā is long,
Add the "e" to make it long.
ă for "man and ā for "mane,"
ă for "can" and ā for "cane,"
ă is short and ā is long,
Add the "e" to make it long.

Do What You Read

Prepare cards describing various activities (e.g., "Open the door," "Walk around the room," "Jump up and down," "Hop on one foot.") The children take turns coming to the front of the room, selecting a card and acting out, to the beat of a drum or tambourine, the activity described on the card.

Read the Words of a Song

Prepare a chart or project a transparency on which is printed the text of a song the class is learning. As they sing, have one of the children point to the words. This will provide practice in several aspects of reading: moving from left to right, moving from one line to the next, relating the image of the word to its sound, and becoming aware of syllables as each one is sung on a different tone.

Add Rhythm Instruments and Sound Effects to Poems and Stories

Have the children read poems and short stories aloud, deciding which rhythm instruments and sound effects can be used to accompany the readings. Then divide the class into groups—some reciting, some reading aloud, and some playing the instruments. Some possibilities are:

Rain—quick, light tapping on tone blocks

Thunder—cymbal crashes

Starry night—triangles, finger cymbals

Horses galloping or trotting—tone blocks, rhythm sticks

Sleigh bells—jingle bells

Indians—tom-toms

Wind—Syllable "ooh" spoken with rising and falling pitch

Rescue scene—bugle call, performed on kazoos

Water rippling—sliding of mallet up and down on song bells

Clock—rhythmic tapping of rhythm sticks

Church bells—resonator bells

Children playing—voices, maracas, tambourines

Hallowe'en—cymbals played softly, then sudden crash

Sad mood—minor chords played on autoharp

Happy mood—skipping rhythms played on black bars of song bells

Your class should be able to think of many other sound effects.

Have a Music Folder

Distribute song sheets with the texts of songs that the class will learn and place them in a music folder. When the children sing the songs, if they have not yet memorized the words, they can read and follow them from the song sheet.

(Some children are more highly motivated to read the words of songs than they are to read from any of their books!)

Have a Song Vocabulary List

Always explain the meanings of new words in songs. You can have the children keep a "Song Vocabulary" list. Some words that might be included from "America, the Beautiful" might be: "spacious," "amber," "fruited," "plain," "grace," "shed." (This could also avoid those situations described in the story of the little boy who prayed, "Lead us not into Penn Station," or of the children who sing, "My country, tears of thee..")

Tape Background Music for Poems and Stories

Have the class listen to several recordings to decide which ones would provide suitable background music for selected poems and stories. Include for their choice music that can suggest the mood of the poem or story. Tape the portions of the selected music and play it as the poems are recited or portions of the story are read aloud.

Listen to Program Music Suggested by Stories and Plays

Have the class read stories which inspired musical compositions (or read to them, or prepare summaries of the stories). Then, play the composition based on the story and have the class discuss the way in which the music expresses the story.

Some literary works which have inspired music are:

Musical Composition	Based On
Omphala's Spinning Wheel, by Saint-Saëns	Greek myth
Romeo and Juliet by Tchaikowsky	Shakespeare's play
Cinderella, ballet by Prokofiev	Fairy tale
Scheherezade, by Rimsky-Korsakoff	"Arabian Nights"
Peer Gynt Suite, by Grieg	Ibsen's play
Incidental music for *A Midsummer Night's Dream,* by Mendelssohn	Shakespeare's play
Mother Goose Suite, by Ravel	Fairy tales ("Beauty and the Beast," "Sleeping Beauty," "Hop o' My Thumb," etc.)
Don Quixote, by Richard Strauss	Cervantes' novel
Through the Looking Glass, by Deems Taylor	Lewis Carroll's book
Hansel and Gretel, opera by Humperdinck	Folk tale
Tale of a Soldier, by Stravinsky	Russian folk tale
The Sleeping Beauty, ballet by Tchaikowsky	Fairy tale

Write About Music

Use topics dealing with music as possible subjects for compositions. Some could be:

1. My Favorite Singer
2. How the First String Instrument (or wind, or percussion) Was Made (Have the children make up their own legends.)
3. Where I Think Music Came From
4. I Am a Drum
5. If There Were No Music

Make a Collection of Music Legends for a Scrapbook or Bulletin Board

Have the pupils do individual research to find legends and fairy tales about music. Have them write brief summaries of the stories and illustrate them with drawings or paintings. Paste these into a class "Scrapbook of Music Legends" or onto a "Music Legends" Bulletin Board.

Some fairy tales and legends about music include:

The Pied Piper (folk tale)

Orpheus and Eurydice (Greek legend)

The Pipes of Pan (Greek legend)

Apollo and the Lyre (Greek legend about the first stringed instrument)

The Soldier's Tale (Russian folk tale about a magic violin)

The Drummer Boy (Christmas story)

The Magic Flute (story of Mozart's opera)

Ulysses and the Sirens (from Homer's *Odyssey)*

Saul and David (from the Bible)

Notice that most of these legends and tales deal with the power of music.

Write Reports About Musicians

Encourage the pupils to bring in articles and news stories about their favorite entertainers and musicians. Have them write summaries of these items to read to the class and include them in your daily news summaries.

Review a TV Music Program

Keep the class informed about music programs on TV—ballets such as *The Nutcracker, Sleeping Beauty, Giselle, Petrouchka, The Green Table,* suitable operas or operettas or films made from musicals such as *West Side Story, The King and I, South Pacific;* stories about musicians, etc. Encourage them to watch and write reviews of these programs.

Monitor TV Background Music

Ask the pupils to notice the background music played during their favorite TV programs. Ask them to determine whether the music affects the mood of the story and what musical devices the composer used to achieve these results.

Write a Book Review About Books Dealing with Music

Have the pupils read books about the lives of musicians or about music and write book reviews about them.

Write a Radio Dramatization

Have the class write and prepare a tape recording or radio program dramatizing incidents in the life of a composer (Mozart's and Beethoven's biographies, because of the extraordinary circumstances of their lives, are of special interest) and incorporate some of his music.

Write a Music Dramatization of a Legend

Have the class write a dramatization of one of the legends or folk tales about music which they have found through research. Have them incorporate rhythm instruments, word chants, and sound effects in the dramatization and then either tape it or perform it over the school radio.

ART

Just as art can be used to enhance the study of music when learning such concepts as musical form or dynamics, or in creating sound scores or drawings dealing with music stories, music can be used to enhance lessons in art—from developing the recognition of colors to inspiring the creation of art works.

Sing a Song About Color

Matching colors takes place whenever color coding is used in playing the autoharp or the Swiss Melody Bells. Several songs can add to the fun.

WHAT IS BILLY WEARING?

Sing additional verses about other children and other colors—Patty's wearing white sneakers, Darryl's wearing a blue shirt, and so on.

WON'T YOU SIT DOWN, LORD

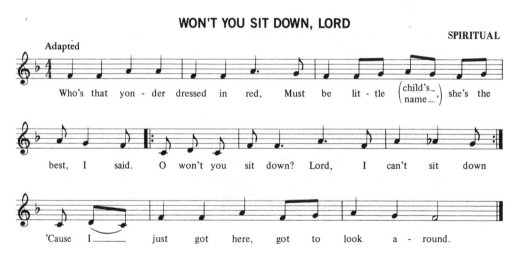

Improvise additional verses based on colors children are wearing.

...dressed in green ... best I've seen.

...dressed in brown ... greatest in town.

...dressed in white ... she's all right.

Draw to Illustrate a Cumulative Song

A cumulative song adds a new verse with each repetition. As "A Tree in the Woods" is sung, draw on the chalkboard to illustrate the "growing" song. (You could have prepared drawings for each addition, but children find it fascinating to watch the development of the story.) You can also have the children draw their own versions of the song.

THE TREE IN THE WOODS

ENGLISH FOLK SONG

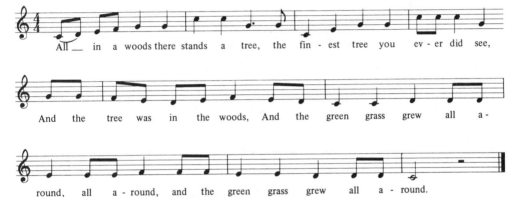

All — in a woods there stands a tree, the fin - est tree you ev - er did see,

And the tree was in the woods, And the green grass grew all a -

round, all a - round, and the green grass grew all a - round.

Verse 2: All in a woods there stands a tree,
The finest tree you ever did see,
And a limb was on the tree, and
the tree was in the woods,
And the green grass grew. . . .

Verse 3: And a branch was on the limb,
and the limb was on the tree, and
the tree was in the woods. . .

Verse 4: And a nest was on the branch, and
the branch was on the limb. . .

Verse 5: And an egg was in the nest, and
the nest was on the branch. . .

Verse 6: And a bird was on the egg. . .

Verse 7: And a wing was on the bird. . .

Verse 8: And a feather was on the wing. . .

Verse 9: And a spot was on the feather. . .

THE TREE IN THE WOODS

Your finished drawing might look something like the illustration. The idea is to have one drawing to which, at each verse, a new part is added.

Verse 1: Draw the tree.

Verse 2: Add a limb to the tree.

Verse 3: Add the branch

Verse 4: Add the nest.

Verse 5: Add the egg.

Verse 6: Add the bird.

Verse 7: Add the wing.

Verse 8: Add a feather.

Verse 9: Add the spot.

Verse 10: ?? Have the class think of other things to add.

The same thing can be done with the cumulative song "There's a Hole in the Bottom of the Sea."

THERE'S A HOLE IN THE BOTTOM OF THE SEA

TRADITIONAL

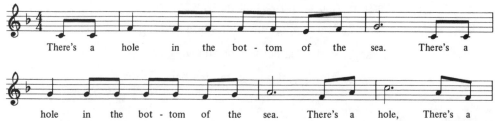

There's   a   hole   in   the   bot - tom   of   the   sea.   There's   a

hole   in   the   bot - tom   of   the   sea.   There's   a   hole,   There's   a

hole, There's a hole in the bot - tom of the sea.

Verse 2: There's a log on the hole in the
bottom of the sea...

Verse 3: There's a bump on the log on the
hole in the bottom of the sea...

Verse 4: There's a frog on the bump on the
log on the hole in the bottom...

Verse 5: There's a leg on the frog on the
bump on the log on the hole...

Verse 6: There's a spot on the leg on the
frog on the bump on the log on
the hole...

Verse 7: There's a speck on the spot on the
leg on the frog on the bump...

Draw or Paint to Music

Without giving the title or any information about the music, play a recording of a composition for the class and have them draw or paint as the music is heard. Let whatever is felt or thought be expressed without any guidance from you. Other activities have called upon the pupils to express dynamics, musical form, or music stories. In this case, complete freedom of self-expression is the goal.

Draw or Paint Sets and Costumes for Music Stories

Any story in music can be the starting point for designing sets for the scenery or costumes for the characters in the story.

Make Puppets for a Music Story

Have the pupils design and make puppets to represent the characters in a music story (e.g., Wolf, Duck, Cat, Hunters, Peter, Grandfather, Bird from *Peter and the Wolf*; Tubby, the frog, the conductor, and the musical instruments for *Tubby the Tuba*).

Act a Puppet Music Play

Have the pupils design background sets and manipulate the puppets to act out the music story as the music is played.

Design Masks to Express Moods of Music

As music is played, have the pupils design and make face masks to represent their feelings and/or the moods of the music.

Select Pictures to Illustrate the Mood of the Music.

Distribute several pictures of varying moods or showing different scenes. Have the class listen to a recording and select the picture which best illustrates the music.

Draw to Illustrate Program Music

Any program music (see Chapter 5) can be used as the basis for drawing or painting illustrations of the story or scenes depicted in the music.

Draw to Illustrate Music Concepts

In addition to expressing dynamics or form by drawing, various other aspects of music can be diagrammed or illustrated by the pupils.

1. Staccato—detached; played in an abruptly separated manner. Legato—smooth and connected.

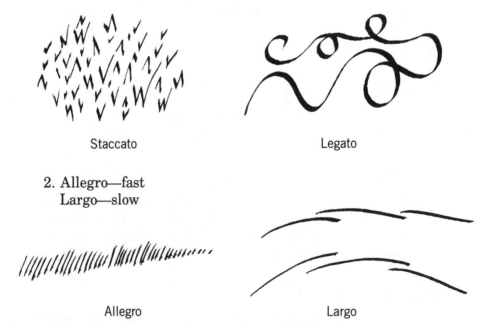

Staccato   Legato

2. Allegro—fast
   Largo—slow

Allegro   Largo

Find ABA Form in Architecture or Art

Have the pupils look for examples of ABA form in architecture, interior decoration or paintings. Examples should illustrate formal balance—one unit in the center of the picture or building with two equal or similar units on each side (pictures of the Capitol in Washington, the Taj Mahal, of a still life showing a bowl of fruit centered on a table).

Design Musical Gift-Wrap Paper

Give the pupils sheets of plain brown paper and have them design gift-wrap paper using any medium they prefer—crayons, pencil, paint, chalk. Have them base the design on musical symbols or pictures of instruments. (See the illustration.)

Make a Music Folder

Give the pupils large sheets of construction paper and have them fold them in half, printing the words "Music Folder" on the front. Let them decorate the covers any way they wish. Have them put into the folders any work sheets, song sheets, or papers from the music period.

Make a Music–Art Bulletin Board

Have the pupils bring in any prints, drawings, copies of paintings, illustrations of sculpture, cartoons they can find which deal with the subject of music, and place them on a "Music in Art" bulletin board.

Relate Style in Music to Style in Art

This activity is suggested for pupils who have had much experience in listening to and learning about music.

Bring in prints illustrating various styles in Art—avant-garde,

Impressionist, Romantic, Baroque. Play recordings of short works from each period and have the class decide which style of music can best be matched with the style of each picture.

Draw or Paint to Illustrate Dances

Play a variety of dance music for the class—disco, ragtime, a tarentella, tango, minuet, hora. Explain and demonstrate, or have some pupils demonstrate, each type of dance. Then have the pupils select and paint pictures to express one or more of the dances. Display the pictures and see if the pupils can guess which dances their classmates have chosen to illustrate.

MATHEMATICS

Count the Drum Beats

Sing the following tune:

Lis - ten   to   me   play   the   drum.   Count   the   times   it   says "rum - tum."

Then play the drum several times as the children count aloud the number of beats:

Drum beats: ✗   ✗   ✗   ✗   ✗

Children: One!   Two!   Three!   Four!   Five!

The children then echo the number of beats they heard by clapping their hands. Repeat the activity playing the drum a different number of beats each time.

Sing Counting Songs

There are many songs that can be used to reinforce mathematics skills such as rote counting, subtraction, addition, or multiplication. Here are some rote counting songs:

THIS OLD MAN

ENGLISH FOLK SONG

This   old   man,   he   played   one,   He   played   nick - nack   on   his   drum.

Nick-nack pad-dy whack, Give a dog a bone, This old man came roll-ing home.

Verse 2: This old man, he played two,
He played nick-nack on his shoe...

Verse 3: This old man, he played three,
He played nick-nack on his tree...

Verse 4: This old man, he played four,
He played nick-nack on his door...

Verse 5: This old man, he played five,
He played nick-nack on his hive...

Have the children make up their own rhymes for each verse. Continue the song, adding another number with each verse.

TEN IN THE BED

TRADITIONAL

There were ten in the bed and the mid-dle one said, "Roll o-ver;

roll o-ver." So they all rolled o-ver and one fell out, there were

nine in the bed and the mid-dle one said, "Roll o-ver, roll o-ver."

So they all rolled o-ver and one fell out, there were eight in the bed...

When you've reached "There were none in the bed," you can start to sing, "Roll back! Roll Back!" and then go on and on and on...

Use a Counting Song to Reinforce Number Recognition

Prepare a series of cards, each of which shows a different number of objects or shapes (e.g., one cat, two stars, three beats, four dogs, five circles, six triangles). Have the children sing "This Old Man," but instead of starting with "This old man, he played *one*.." hold up one of the picture cards in random order. The children determine the number of objects on the card and accordingly sing the appropriate verse.

Card shown: ○ ○ ○ ○ ○
Class sings: "...he played five.."

Card shown: ✳   ✳
Class sings: "...he played two.."

Play the Drum the Correct Number of Counts

Using the prepared cards showing a different number of objects on each card, hold them up one at a time in random order. The children take turns playing on the drum the number of objects they see drawn on the cards.

Play the Digit on the Drum

Prepare cards showing digits from one to ten. Hold them up, one at a time, in random order. The children take turns playing the drum the number of times indicated by the digit.

Use Bells to Tell Time

When young children are learning to tell time, have a series of drawings of clock faces showing different hours. Have the children take turns "playing" the time on the song bells or resonator bells—two tones for two o'clock, eleven tones for eleven o'clock, etc. If the black bars of the instruments are used, some lovely pentatonic melodies could result.

Use the Drum in Teaching the Symbols for "More Than" And "Less Than"

Place a number of different rhythm instruments on a table and give each of two volunteers an instrument. On the chalkboard, write the symbols $>$ and $<$. The first child plays from one to five beats on his or her instrument. Then, point to one of the symbols and have the second child play his or her instrument one more or one less time, according to the symbol indicated. Repeat this several times with different children.

Guess Whether There Are the Same, More, or Less Beats

On the chalkboard, write <, >, and = and let two children select rhythm instruments. As the class mentally counts, the first child plays any number of beats from one to five (or up to any amount you think appropriate). The second child then plays his or her instrument for less, more, or the same number of beats. Call on a third child to indicate which of the three signs—<, >, or =—was heard.

Play Rhythm Band Addition

Give two children different instruments. Have a series of addition problems on the board.

Drum		Rhythm Sticks	= Number of Beats
4	plus	3	
5	plus	2	
6	plus	4	
7	plus	5	

For the first example, the drummer beats the drum four times and then the second child plays the rhythm sticks three times while the class counts the total number of beats they hear. Have another child write the sum on the board. Continue the activity, letting different children play the drum and sticks for each example.

Add the Note Durations

When doing arithmetic problems, include examples showing notes. The children write the duration value of each note and then add the counts to find the total in each measure; or, they can add the total number of counts in several measures.

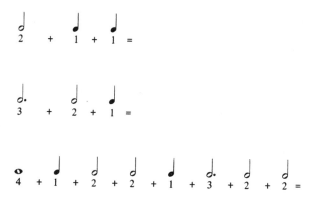

2 + 1 + 1 =

3 + 2 + 1 =

4 + 1 + 2 + 2 + 1 + 3 + 2 + 2 =

Sense Fractions Through Body Movement

Have half of the class clap quarter notes while the rest of the class stamps half notes. Have them listen to the result and ask, "How many quarters do you *hear* adding up to one half note?"

Have the children tap the quarter notes with one hand as they stamp whole notes. Ask, "How many quarters do you *feel* adding up to one whole?"

You can do the same activities combining half and whole notes, eighth and half notes, quarter and eighth notes. In addition to the usual activities involving visual experiences, the children will thus *hear* and *feel* fractional relationships.

Use Rhythm Notation in Fraction Examples

When studying fractions, use whole, half, quarter, and eighth notes in addition examples.

$$\frac{1}{2} + \frac{2}{4} + \frac{2}{8} =$$

$$\frac{3}{8} + \frac{1}{4} + \frac{1}{8} = \frac{?}{8}$$

$$\frac{1}{2} + \frac{1}{4} + \frac{1}{2} + \frac{1}{2} =$$

$$\frac{2}{2} = ?$$

Add Sets Using Movement

Movement and sound can help children to *hear* and to *feel* addition. Ask several children to form two groups. Place some problems on the chalkboard showing sets, as follows:

CLAP	STAMP
(Group One)	(Group Two)
1. ☆ ☆	✳ ✳ ✳ ✳
2. △ △ △ △ △	X X X X X
3. 3	7

Group One claps, then Group Two stamps the number of times indicated in the first example while the rest of the class adds the total number of beats. Continue the activity, using different children to move to and perform the other examples.

Play the Multiplication Table

Place all of your rhythm instruments on a table. As the class repeatedly chants "2 × 1 = 2," two of the children come to the front of the room, select instruments, and play them to the rhythm of the chant. Then each of these children selects another child, and the four play instruments as the class chants, "2 × 2 = 4." each of the four children picks others to join them and the eight play. This continues ("2 × 8 = 16"; "2 × 16 = 32") until the whole class is involved.

Play Musical Metrics

Have a number of small objects. Have the children stand in a circle and start to play a recording. The children pass one of the objects around the circle until the music is stopped. The child holding the object has to guess its metric weight or length and the answer is checked using a metric scale or ruler.

Repeat this activity a number of times, using different objects.

The same sort of game can be played using, instead of objects, cards on which various arithmetic examples—simple multiplication, division, addition, or subtraction problems—are placed.

Do Music Note Division Examples

Use notes of various durations in division problems. Have the class substitute the duration value of the note for the symbol and then proceed with the division problem.

| Examples | Answers |

$$\frac{\circ}{2} = \qquad \frac{\circ}{2} = \frac{4}{2} = 2$$

$$\frac{16}{\circ} = \qquad \frac{16}{\circ} = \frac{16}{4} = 4$$

$$\frac{\circ}{3} = \qquad \frac{\circ}{3} = \frac{4}{3} = 1\frac{1}{3}$$

SCIENCE

Sing to Learn the Parts of the Body

There's "Hokey-Pokey," of course. Another well-known song-game is the "Exercise Song" to the tune of "There Is a Tavern in the

Town." Each time the song is repeated, the movements are continued and the name of one more part of the body is omitted. Finally, the group is exercising as they just "think" the words.

HEAD, SHOULDERS, KNEES AND TOES

SONG GAME

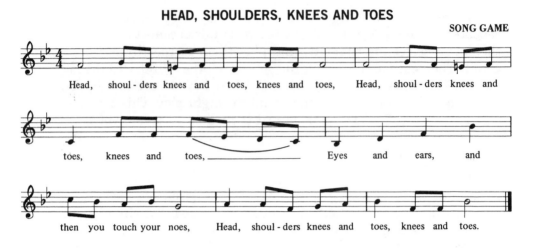

Sing a Weather Song

Occasionally, when the daily news report is given, have the class sing an appropriate song to describe the weather.

A lovely, sunshiny day—"Oh, What a Beautiful Morning."

A rainy day—"Raindrops Keep Falling on My Head" (or, for little children, the children's chant, "It's raining, it's pouring, the old man is snoring.")

Snow—"Jingle Bells"

A hot, lazy day—"Summertime," from *Porgy and Bess*.

Have a Musical Weather Forecast

If you include the weather forecast in your daily news report, this can be done by having a small group of children serve as a "committee" to present the forecast using sound effects, noises, voices, and rhythm instruments while the rest of the class tries to guess what the weather will be.

A storm—cymbals, maracas, drum, voices representing the wind chanting "ooh———" with rising and falling inflections.

Snow—jingle bells, voices saying "ssh, ssh, ssh, ...," triangles.

Let the children use their imaginations to create the sound effects.

Sing About Farm Animals

"Old McDonald Had a Farm" is enjoyed by many groups of different ages. In early childhood classes, this song, accompanied by pictures of the animals, can be used to reinforce learning about farm animals.

Listen to Music About Animals

Enhance lessons about animals by playing selections from some of the following compositions. Let the class try to decide what characteristics of the animals are represented by the composer.

Carnival of the Animals by Saint-Saëns—lion, kangaroos, fish, birds ("Aviary"), "Cuckoo in the Deep Woods," turtle, elephant, swan.

"Flight of the Bumble Bee," by Rimsky-Korsakoff.

Adventures of a Zoo, by Kleinsinger—kangaroo, elephant, mouse, hippopotamus, monkey.

"Lark Song," from *Scenes of Youth,* by Tchaikowsky.

Listen to Music Depicting Nature

Enrich lessons about our earth and its place in the universe by playing works such as *The Planets,* by Holst; *La Mer,* (The Sea) by Debussy; "To the Rising Sun," by Torjussen; "Clair de Lune," by Debussy.

Use Musical Instruments to Demonstrate Sound Vibrations

1. Strike a tuning fork or triangle and immediately plunge it into a basin of water. The movement of the water will illustrate through the sense of sight that sound is caused by vibrations.

2. Let each child in the class touch the triangle or cymbal immediately after it is played. They will *feel* the vibrations which have created the sound.

Demonstrate the Relationship of the Length of a String to Its Pitch

Pluck the lowest string of a guitar. The children will see it vibrate and hear the low pitch. Now place one finger at the midpoint of the string and pluck it again. Because only half of the string will be vibrating, the tone should be one octave higher. This will demonstrate that (1) the shorter the string, the higher the pitch and (2) one string twice the length of a second will sound one octave lower in pitch than the second.

Create an Electronic Composition

Tape voices and other environmental sounds as well as the sounds made by musical instruments. Play them back at various speeds as you record them on a second tape recorder. The pitch will be distorted—higher at the faster speed, lower at the slower speed. This will demonstrate that faster vibrations result in higher pitch and slower vibrations result in lower pitch.

The same fact can be demonstrated by playing a 45 rpm recording at 78 rpm or 33 rpm.

This activity can also provide a planned creative experience for the class.

Invent a Musical Instrument

After the children have discovered that musical sounds can be made by blowing, banging, plucking, bowing, or shaking various instruments, they can try to invent their own instruments using "found" materials.

Demonstrate the Relationship of Pitch to Length of Sounding Column

Play the lowest tone on a recorder or tonette by blowing into it with all the holes closed. Explain that the air is coming out of the bottom of the instrument. Release all the holes and blow again. Explain that the air is now coming out of the highest hole. The pitch of the tone will be much higher. This demonstration will enable the class to observe that when the column is longer, the pitch is lower.

SOCIAL STUDIES

The variety of music that can be incorporated into the Social Studies lesson is as great as the variety of experiences in the history of Man. If music has been called the "universal language," it is because although different melodies, rhythms, and tone qualities may be used, the same emotions and experiences common to all people are expressed. Family relationships, mother love, love of home and country, romantic love, faith, humor, struggle, work, sorrow, loneliness, suffering, and joy—all of these find their outlet in music.

Every period in history has had its own music. Every country has its own songs and dances. There are peoples in Man's history who have had no graven images. Some have had no written literature; some, no paintings or drawings or formalized architecture. All have had music.

That is why, if we are to really understand the story of Man, it is essential to know his music.

Listen to Music About America

Many composers have been inspired by the ideals of the United States and the events in its history. There are many such works to which your class can listen when studying these aspects. In the case of the "musicals," the pupils can learn some of the songs and sing along with the recordings.

Early History (Indians)

McDowell, *Indian Suite,* No. 2; one of the few orchestral works inspired by Indian lore and using Indian themes.

Recordings of the music of American Indians.

Early Settlements

Caillet, *Variations on Pop Goes the Weasel;* based on the Early American song-game.

Phillips, *John Alden and Priscilla.*

Phillips, *Selections from McGuffey's Readers.*

Weill, *Knickerbocker Holiday,* a musical story of early settlers in old New York.

Revolutionary Period

Ives, *A New England Tryptich,* based on the music of the first major American composer, William Billings (1746-1800).

Phillips, *Moonlight Ride of Paul Revere.*

Civil War

Copland, *A Lincoln Portrait;* an inspired tribute incorporating words of this great president.

Gould, *American Salute;* a series of variations on the Civil War song, "When Johnny Comes Marching Home Again."

Harris, *Abraham Lincoln Walks at Midnight.*

Expansion Westward

Bergsma, *Paul Bunyan Suite;* inspired by the "tall tales" about the American folk hero.

Berlin, *Annie, Get Your Gun;* musical comedy about Buffalo Bill and Annie Oakley.

Copland, *Billy the Kid,* ballet suite; based on the life of the famous outlaw.

Copland, *Rodeo,* ballet suite; a celebration of the spirit of the frontier.

Rodgers, *Oklahoma!;* the well-known musical about the farmers and the ranchers, their social customs, and ideals.

Thomson, *The Plough That Broke the Plains;* music from the motion picture.

Black History (Works by Afro-Americans)

Recordings of "blues," especially those of W.C. Handy.

Recordings of "ragtime," especially pieces by Joplin.

These turn-of-the-century favorites had a profound effect on the history of American music.

Dett, "Juba Dance"; suggested by the "Juba" style of dancing. "Juba" was one of the finest dancers of the 1820's. Charles Dickens saw him perform and wrote enthusiastically about this great black dancer.

Gottschalk, "Cakewalk." In the days of slavery, contests were held on the plantations to see which slave could spill the least amount of water while dancing with a pail of water on his head. A high, strutting step was used and the prize was a cake. Hence, the "cakewalk."

Joplin, *Treemonisha;* selections from the opera about a Negro teacher and her aspirations for her people.

Still, *Afro-American* Symphony incorporates ideas from jazz and the blues.

Still, *From the Black Belt.*

Still, *Pages from Negro History.*

Recordings of spirituals, gospel songs, and of such performers as Marion Anderson, Louis Armstrong, Leontyne Price, Sammy Davis, Jr., Duke Ellington, "Fats" Waller, Paul Robeson.

In addition to the above compositions, Gershwin's opera *Porgy and Bess* deals with life in the "Catfish Row" section of Charleston, South Carolina.

Second World War

Rodgers, *South Pacific;* musical about the humor, courage, problems and heartaches of a group of American men in uniform stationed in the South Pacific.

Rodgers, *Victory at Sea;* music from the motion picture.

The Recent Scene

Bernstein, *West Side Story;* a serious music drama presenting the tragic results of ethnic division.

Bock, *Fiorello;* the story of New York's colorful mayor La Guardia and his fight against municipal corruption.

Carpenter, *Skyscrapers;* ballet about modern urban life.

Lane, *Finian's Rainbow;* musical comedy dealing with racism in the South.

Pictures of America

Copland, *Appalachian Spring;* inspired by the farmers and settlers of Appalachia and written for Martha Graham and her dance group. The music incorporates the famous Shaker, melody, "Simple Gifts."

Grofé, *Death Valley Suite*
Grand Canyon Suite
Hudson River Suite
Mississippi Suite

These works present paintings in music of scenes from these areas. The best known selection is "On the Trail," from *The Grand Canyon Suite.*

Schuman, *George Washington Bridge.*

Thomson, "The Alligator and the 'Coon," from *Louisiana Story* (motion picture); the story in music of a young boy, his pet raccoon, and an alligator. It is set in the swamps of Louisiana.

The Ideals of America

Bloch, *America;* a large, magnificent work employing symphony orchestra and using American folk songs, hymns, and jazz.

Copland, *Fanfare for the Common Man;* a stirring work, hailing the entrance of Everyman.

Ives, *Three Places in New England*
> "The 'St. Gaudens' in Boston Common"

> "Colonel Shaw and His Colored Regiment"; a depiction of the pain courage, and determination of Civil War troops.

> "Putnam's Camp, Redding, Connecticut"; story of a young boy who meets the spirit of the Goddess of Liberty. The work recalls the sacrifices of the American Revolution and the ideals of the rebels. The music combines patriotic band music, popular songs, and original composition.

Robeson, *Ballad for Americans;* a choral work based on the history of America in song and narration. It stresses the struggle for human and civil rights.

Sousa, "Stars and Stripes Forever," "Washington Post March"; exemplifying patriotism—pride and love of country.

Folk Songs

Among the finest folk song collections are those of Burl Ives, Woody Guthrie, Pete Seeger, The Weavers, John Lomax, and Harry Belafonte.

Sing a Song of History

Almost every period, region, and development in American history has had its own songs. As the pupils learn about these events and historic periods, teach the simple folk songs sung by the people of those times. The students will have occasion to remember and sing them throughout their lives.

Following are a small percentage of those you can find in numerous collections of American and world-wide folk song books, school music books, and children's song books. They have been selected not only because they are representative of periods and regions in American history, but also because they bring greater understanding of and illumine the events and lives of the people in the story of the United States. The source is listed after each song, with full bibliographical information given at the end of the chapter.

Songs of American Indians

Corn Grinding Song: The Navahos settled more than 100 years ago in the area of Arizona and New Mexico. Music accompanied many aspects of their daily lives. Corn was ground by rolling small stones over the kernels of corn which were placed in a large hollowed-out stone. This work was performed to the rhythm of the "Corn Grinding Song." (*Expressing Music.*)

Ghost Dance Song: The Arapaho Indians used to live in what is now Wyoming and Colorado. This dance was a symbol of peace and could last for 5 days with as many as 500 braves taking part. (*Expressing Music.*)

Indian Lullaby: The universality of mother love and the gentle rhythms and tender melodies of lullabies are highlighted in this song. (*Expressing Music.*)

Navaho Happy Song: The steady rhythms and pentatonic melody (the five tones used are C,D,E,G,A) are typical of Indian melodies. (*Discovering Music Together,* Book 5: *Discovering Music Together, Teacher Education Edition.*)

Songs of the Early Settlers

Old Hundredth: One of the Pilgrim's favorite psalms, "Old Hundredth" was brought here from Europe. A song dating back to as early as the sixteenth century, it was typical of religious music of the Puritans who, although they frowned on secular music, considered psalms an important part of worship. (*Fireside Book of Folk Songs;* "Experiencing Music.").

We Gather Together: The melody of this song is of Dutch origin and it became one of the hymns of early settlers from Holland. (*Sing Together Children; Pocket Full of Songs; Experiencing Music; Making Music Your Own,* Book 5; *Making Music Your Own,* Book 4.)

Songs of the American Revolution

Chester: William Billings wrote this song for the troops of Washington's army. It reaffirms their determination to win freedom for the colonies. (*Travellin' On With the Weavers; Making Music Your Own,* Book 5.)

Johnnie Has Gone for a Soldier (Buttermilk Hill): A sweet pensive song in which a young girl expresses her longing for her sweetheart who has "gone for a soldier" to serve in the colonial forces. (*Git On Board—Folk Songs for Group Singing; Fireside Book of Folk Songs; Travellin' On With the Weavers, Pointer System for Guitar; Making Music Your Own,* Book 5.)

Riflemen of Bennington: A lively "pep song" of the Continental troops, the words telling of the coming victory, (*Git On Board; Making Music Your Own,* Book 5.)

Yankee Doodle: Originally, "Yankee Doodle" was a song of the

British army mocking the motley, disorganized, shabby American soldiers. Later, the Americans adopted the tune and, turning the tables, sang it in triumph at Burgoyne's surrender. (*Making Music Your Own*, Book 4; *Making Music Your Own*, Book 3; *Expressing Music.*)

The Expansion of the United States

Betsy From Pike: This ballad tells, in lilting melody and with light humor, of the trials and tribulations of those who, during the Gold Rush, crossed the country to reach California. (*Discovering Music Together*, Book 5; *Singing With Children; Fireside Book of Folk Songs; American Song Bag.*)

Drill Ye Tarriers: The tarriers were workers who labored alongside the steam drills to remove the loose rocks. This is another example of a humorous treatment of difficult situations. (*American Song Bag; Git on Board*)

Elanoy: This song, with its melody harking back to Irish tunes, praises the beauty and the promise of "Elanoy." Like the immigrants who came to America, the pioneers who went to Illinois had the same hope for a better life for, says the song, if you "move your family westward, good health you will enjoy and rise to wealth and honor." (*American Song Bag.*)

Erie Canal (I've Got a Mule; Fifty Miles on the Erie Canal): The Erie Canal opened in 1825, connecting Albany to Buffalo. This lively, humorous song celebrates the mules that towed the barges and the men who navigated this canal which opened up a new passageway for those who wanted to travel North towards the Great Lakes. (*Git On Board; Discovering Music Together*, Book 5; *Fireside Book of Folk Songs; American Song Bag; Singing With Children; Pocket Full of Songs, One Song More; Melodies for Music Makers.*)

I've Been Working on the Railroad: This lively, rhythmic old American work song is probably the best known of its type. (*Making Music Your Own*, Book 3; *Fireside Book of Folk Songs; Pointer System for Guitar.*)

John Henry: The driving, swinging rhythm of this song sets the beat for the swinging hammers of the railroad workers and chain gangs of the South. John Henry tells the legend of the man who competed with a steam drill to prove that a man was better than a machine. He won—but died in the attempt. (*Fireside Book of Folk Songs; Making Music Your Own*, Book 6; *Expressing Music; American Song Bag; Git On Board; Discovering Music Together*, Book 5; *Songs of Man; Pointer System for Guitar.*)

Little Old Sod Shanty: This tuneful song describes the living conditions of the first pioneers who tackled life on the prairies of the Great Plains. (*American Song Bag; Pointer System for Guitar.*)

Paddy Works on the Erie (Working on the Railroad; Patsy-Ory-Ay; Fillee-Mi-Orri-Orri-Ay): This is a humorous song recounting the adventures of the Irish workers who helped to build our railroads. (*Git on Board; Travellin' On With the Weavers*)

Polly-Wolly Doodle: As America grew, traffic between North and South grew with it. The Mississippi River boats took thousands of passengers from North to South and "Polly-Wolly-Doodle" is typical of the entertainment songs that were performed by minstrel groups on board the ship. (*Making Music Your Own*, Book 3; *Pointer System for Guitar.*)

Songs of the Sailors

In the eighteenth century, American ships sailed the seas in search of trade. As the sailors on board the great sailing vessels went about their tasks, they sang "chanties" to accompany and ease their work—hauling up the anchor, furling and raising sails, and winding rope around the "capstan." Among the best known and loved of these work songs are:

Blow the Man Down: (Fireside Book of Folk Songs; American Song Bag; One Tune More; Pointer System for Guitar; Making Music your Own, Book 5.)

Drunken Sailor: (Fireside Book of Folk Songs; Pointer System for Guitar.)

Goodbye, My Lover (Bye-Low, My Baby); (Melodies for Music Makers.)

Shenandoah: A leader would sing a solo and the men responded in song as they rhythmically labored. (*Fireside Book of Folk Songs; Work and Sing.)*

Songs of the Civil War

Battle Hymn of the Republic: Written by Julia Ward Howe, this became the marching song of the Northern armies. (*Fireside Book of Folk Songs; Singing With Children; Making Music Your Own*, Book 3.)

Blue Tail Fly: This song was composed by the famous minstrel, Daniel Emmett. It is said to have been one of Abraham Lincoln's favorites. (*Singing With Children; Fireside Book of Folk Songs; Making Music Your Own*, Book 3.)

Goober Peas: "Goober peas" are peanuts and this humorous, ironic, tuneful song of the Confederate Army describes the soldiers sitting by the roadside eating goober peas as they long for the war to be over. (*Discovering Music Together,* Book 5: *Songs of Man; Singing With Children.*)

John Brown's Body: Set to "Battle Hymn of the Republic," this song celebrates the contributions of John Brown to the struggle against slavery. (*American Song Bag; Fireside Book of Folk Songs.*)

Lincoln and Liberty: During Henry Clay's candidacy, other words were set to this old tune. In this version, it is Lincoln's presidential campaign that is supported. (*American Song Bag.*)

Old Abe Lincoln: This song, to the tune of the "Old Gray Mare" tells the story of the man who "came out of the wilderness" to lead his country and free the slaves. It was sung by Lincoln's supporters. (*Expressing Music*; first stanza only in *American Song Bag; Making Music Your Own,* Book 5.)

Rally Round the Flag: This is a stirring, vigorous call to battle for freedom. (*Travellin' On With the Weavers.*)

When Johnny Comes Marching Home Again: This famous and powerful song was originally an Irish folk song. The melody was adopted and adapted as it became a marching song of the Union Army. (*Travellin' On With the Weavers; Melodies for Music Makers; Fireside Book of Folk Songs; Making Music Your Own,* Book 2; *Singing With Children; Expressing Music.*)

Songs of Afro-American History

Back of the Bus: A song from the days of Martin Luther King, "Back of the Bus" tells in two brief verses the story of the fight for integration in the South. It was written in a prison cell by Mary Jane Pigee, a civil rights demonstrator. (*One in Song.*)

Didn't My Lord Deliver Daniel? This song illustrates the two meanings underlying many of the Negro spirituals. On one level, it is a religious song about bible stories. But it is also a song of deliverance for every man, Canaan representing both the biblical Holy Land and the North where one can find freedom. (*Look Away.*)

Go Down, Moses: A spiritual of the slaves, the song has two dimensions. At the same time that it tells of Moses freeing the Hebrew slaves, it really expresses the prayer to "Let my [own] people go." (*Git on Board; Look Away; Fireside Book of Folk Songs; Singing with Children.*)

Lift Every Voice and Sing: This moving, powerful song by Rosamond Johnson has become the "National Negro Hymn." The words tell of the difficult past and of the hope for future fulfillment. (*Git On Board.*)

Many Thousand Gone (No More Auction Block): This powerful protest song cries out against slavery as it declares, "No more auction block for me ... no more driver's lash." *(Songs of Man; One in Song; Fireside Book of Folk Songs.)*

Nobody Knows the Trouble I've Seen: Perhaps no other Negro Spiritual so poignantly expresses the anguish of slavery. *(Fireside Book of Folk Songs; Singing With Children; Joyful Singing; Look Away.)*

Swing Low, Sweet Chariot: Ostensibly singing about the "chariot" coming "over Jordan" to "carry me home" to heaven, this spiritual was also a Freedom song—the chariot, the angels, heaven, symbolizing the underground railroad and the escape to hope for freedom in the North. (See the score for this song in Chapter 6.)

We Shall Overcome: This freedom song became the rallying cry for the 1960's human rights campaign of Martin Luther King. It has become an integral part of his memory. *(One in Song; Great Songs of the Sixties.)*

When the Saints Go Marching In: In New Orleans at the turn of the century, when a funeral procession would start out for the cemetery, solemn hymns would be played by an accompanying band. On the way back from the burial, the music would become livelier and livelier, culminating in this famous, popular song. Life was to go on. *(Making Music Your Own, Book 7; Pointer System for Guitar; Seventy-Two Giants.)*

Songs of the Cowboys and the "Wild West"

Dogie Song (Git Along, Little Dogies (Whoopie-Ti-Yo; As I Was Riding); A cowboy sings to his dogies—calves which have lost their mothers—as he herds his cattle along the trail. The loping rhythms suggest the sound of horses' hooves and the song provides an excellent opportunity for the use of rhythm band accompaniment. *(Expressing Music; Exploring Music, Book 3; Making Music Your Own, Book 4; One Tune More; Travellin' On With the Weavers; Fireside Book of Folk Songs; Singing With Children, American Song Bag; Discovering Music Together, Book 5.)*

Home on the Range: This most famous of all cowboy songs was written by a physician from the Midwest who had never seen a ranch! It may first have been published in the 1870's and succeeds in expressing the loneliness and beauty of the western range. *(Discovering Music Together; Fireside Book of Folk Songs; Singing With Children; Making Music Your Own, Book 6; Exploring Music; Work and Sing.)*

Jesse James: No account of American history would be complete without the story of Jesse James, the fabled bandit. This song, albeit favorable to Mr. James, provides information about his life. (*American Song Bag.*)

Old Texas: The words tell of the conflicting interests of the ranchers who needed wide-open spaces and the farmers who had to fence in their land in order to survive, (Score in Chapter 1.)

The Lone Star Trail: This is a description of the daily life of the Texas cowboy. (*Discovering Music Together,* Book 5; *American Song Bag.*)

Songs of the Farmers

The life of the farmer has also provided subject matter for song.

Boll Weevil: This song tells about some of the problems of the farmer; it deals with a crop destroyer—the little black bug from Mexico who comes "just lookin' for a home." (*Sing Together Children; Song Bag; Songs of Man; Pocket Full of Songs; One Tune More.*)

The Farmer (The Farmer Is the Man): In this ditty, the life of the man "who feeds them all" is described. (*American Song Bag; Joyful Singing; Songs of Man.*)

Songs of the Labor Movement

Joe Hill: Joe Hill, a union organizer, was executed in 1915 on a framed up murder charge. This moving song is a tribute to him. (*Fireside Book of Folk Songs.*)

Which Side Are You On?: The bitter Harlan County coal strike gave birth to this vigorous labor union song by teenager Florence Reece, the daughter of a coal miner. (*Travellin' On With the Weavers.*)

Turn of the Century—Songs of the "Gay Nineties" and Early Twentieth Century

Daisy, Daisy (Daisy Bell; Bicycle Built for Two); This song, with its waltz clog rhythm, describes a favorite mode of transportation of the period. (*Singing With Children; Pocket Full of Songs; Sing Together Children.*)

In My Merry Oldsmobile: America's delight with its newfound automobiles is expressed in this song. (*Pointer System for Guitar.*)

School Days: The words present a picture of the one-room school house—the hickory stick, the "three R's," the calico dresses of the little girls, and the slates upon which the children wrote. (By Gus Edwards, the song is copyrighted by Mills Music, Inc.)

Sidewalks of New York (East Side, West Side); The favorite street games of children of many generations were played on the "sidewalks of [early twentieth century] New York." (*Pointer System for Guitar; Singing With Children; Pocket Full of Songs; One Tune More.*)

Songs of the First World War

Hinkey-Dinkey-Parlez-Vous (Mademoiselle from Armentieres): With some judicious revision and rewriting of the text, this lively song can be an enjoyable one to teach pupils. It was a favorite of the "doughboys" in France during the first World War and illustrates the unbreakable spirit of these young men. (*American Song Bag.*)

Over There: From the musical comedy, *Johnnie Get Your Gun,* this song extolls the American expeditionary forces in France. (By George M. Cohan, the song is copyrighted by Leo Feist.)

Yankee Doodle Dandy: This is another "flag-waving" song of the period written by George M. Cohan. (*Pointer System for Guitar.*)

Hobo Songs

Hallelujah, I'm a Bum: Another side of American history is evidenced by the songs of the hoboes—umemployed people who, especially in times of economic depression, stowed away in box cars to travel the country, "panhandling" along the way. (*Fireside Book of Folk Songs; American Song Bag.*)

King of the Road: A more recent song, "King of the Road" also happily describes the life of the hobo. (*Great Songs of the Sixties.*)

Songs of Our Times

Blowing in the Wind: A peace song of the Vietnam war, the text asks how long before mankind will be united. (*Great Songs of the Sixties.*)

Little Boxes: This song presents a somewhat sardonic view of the regimentation and shallowness of some aspects of modern life. (*Great Songs of the Sixties.*)

The City Blues: A folk "blues," the text tells about how you "really got to know your way" in such big, baffling cities as New York, Chicago, Detroit, New Orleans, and Los Angeles. It is set to the typical altered scale and harmonies of the blues. (*Experiencing Music.*)

Where Have All the Flowers Gone?: Another song expressing the longing for peace. (*Travellin' On With the Weavers; Great Songs of the Sixties.*)

Songs of American Idealism

If I Had a Hammer: The ideal of brotherhood became one of America's dreams as millions of immigrants from all parts of the world met here on common ground. This song is an expression of this aspect of the history of the United States. (*Travellin' On With the Weavers.*)

Oh, Freedom: This traditional song expresses the American ideal of freedom—of preferring death to slavery. (*Travellin' On With the Weavers; One in Song.*)

Simple Gifts: Originating in England in 1747, the Shaker sect established many settlements in the New World. They were called Shakers because of the dancing and shaking movements they made during their religious ceremonies. They believed in a life of simplicity, work, and cooperative effort. The lovely melody of this song was used by Copland in his orchestral work *Appalachian Spring.* (*Expressing Music; Sing Together Children.*)

This Land Is Your Land: A rousing celebration of America, "This Land Is Your Land" exalts the beauty and oneness of our country. (*Singing With Children; Melodies for Music Makers; Travellin' On With the Weavers; Making Music Your Own,* Book 3; *Expressing Music.*)

Some Miscellaneous Songs

Aloha Oe: A beautiful song by Queen Liliuokalani, "Aloha Oe" exemplifies the beauty and friendliness of the people of one of our newest states. (*Discovering Music Together,* Book 4; and Teacher Education Edition, *One Tune More.*)

Praise the Lord and Pass the Ammunition: By Frank Loesser, this song was written in support of the efforts of this country in World War II. It was very popular in its time. (Copyrighted by Famous Music Corporation.)

MISCELLANEOUS ACTIVITIES

Sing the Days of the Week:

This is a good activity song for all levels as well as a pleasant way to review the days of the week. If the pupils eat in a school cafeteria which has a repetitious menu, they can substitute the "foods of the day" for the ones in the song:

TODAY IS MONDAY

TRADITIONAL

To - day　is　Mon - day!　　Mon - day roast beef,　All　you hap - py chil - dren,　we

Friday—fish;
Saturday—chicken;
Sunday—ice cream

Practice Left and Right

As one child beats a drum with the indicated hand and the other children pretend to play, have the class chant;

I play the drum with my right, right, right,
I make a sound which is out of sight.
Left hand, play now with left hand.
Play the drum in the ragtime band.

Left, left, right, right,
Left, right, right.
Left, left, right, right,
Left, right, right.

For the last stanza, when the children become skillful, you can make this a challenging game by changing the order in which the directions are called:

Right, left, left, right,

Right, right, left.

Left, left, right, right,

Right, left, right.

Sing a Song to Practice Left and right

The Hokey-Pokey song-game provides an excellent activity to reinforce the concepts of "left" and "right."

Play "Left, Right, Pass the Button"

Have the children stand in a circle and, as music is played, start to pass a small, soft object to the right around the circle. When you call out, "to the left," they change direction and pass the object to the left. Alternate calling out, "To the left" and "To the right," and stop the music at times. The child holding the object leaves the circle.

Play a Left and Right Circle Game (Early Childhood)

AMERICAN SONG GAME

Cir - cle to the left, old red wag - on, Cir - cle to the left, old red wag - on.

Cir - cle to the left, old red wag - on, Fare you well my dar - ling.

2. Circle to the right, old red wagon...

3. Shake your right hand now, old red wagon...

4. Shake your left hand now...

5. Stamp your left foot now, old red wagon...

6. Stamp your right foot...

7. Wiggle left hip now...

8. Ev'rybody in...

9. Ev'rybody out...

MAINSTREAMING, MUSIC, AND THE CLASSROOM CURRICULUM

Over and over, experiments have shown that children learn better when music is part of the lesson and of the school curriculum. An experimental group of disadvantaged preschool youngsters made significantly fewer errors in recalling stories heard with taped music in the background than did those who heard the same stories without music.[1] Children who were given daily music instruction in music showed greater self-reliance and had improved attendance.[2] Music played in the background during mathematics lessons resulted not only in greater achievement for many of the pupils, but also in more positive student attitudes towards the classes.[3] Also, a number of studies have shown that when music lessons are incorporated into the training of retarded children, their reading scores improve.[4]

All children can benefit from the cultural, intellectual, and aesthetic values of music, from its power to soothe or stimulate, to increase attention, to provide motivation and enjoyment and the opportunity to participate with others and to develop self-esteem.

For many retarded mainstreamed children, however, music is more than beneficial. Nonverbal and slower to grasp intellectual concepts, they can best learn if they have music to bridge the gap between themselves and those words they find so difficult to follow. They can learn more easily and remember more if what is being taught is taught rhythmically and tunefully.

Grasp every opportunity throughout the day to use music in the classroom curriculum. All the pupils will remember more and the classroom will be a joyous one.

---

[1]Arthur Dawkins, "Effects of Music and Instruction on Auditory Discrimination Test Scores of Disadvantaged Pre-School Students." (Unpublished doctoral dissertation, Catholic University of America, 1973.)

[2]Burrel Samuel Hood, "Effect of Daily Instruction in Public School Music and Related Experience Upon Non-Musical Personal and School Attitudes of Average Achieving Third Grade Students." Mississippi State University, 1973.)

[3]Cornell Lane, "The Effects of Three Types of Background Music on Selected Behaviors in an Elementary School Setting." (Unpublished doctoral dissertation, University of Tennessee, 1976.)

[4]Ruth Zinar, "Reading, Writing, and Music," *The New York Teacher*, December 2, 1973, p. 21. Also, "Reading Language and Reading Music," *Music Educators Journal*, March, 1976, pp. 71-74.

BIBLIOGRAPHY
FOR SONGS IN AMERICAN HISTORY

American Song Bag. Carl Sandburg, Editor. New York: Harcourt and Brace, 1927.

Discovering Music Together Series. Chicago: Follett Publishing Company, 1967.

Experiencing Music, from *New Dimensions in Music Series.* New York: American Book Company, 1970.

Exploring Music Series. New York: Holt, Rhinehart and Winston, 1966.

Expressing Music from *New Dimensions in Music Series.* New York: American Book Company, 1970.

Fireside Book of Folk Songs. New York: Simon and Schuster, 1947.

Git on Board; Folk Songs for Group Singing. New York: Edward Marks Company, 1944.

Joyful Singing. Delaware, Ohio: Informal Music Service. Revised, 1962.

Look Away. Delaware, Ohio: Cooperative Music Service, Revised, 1960.

Making Music Your Own Series. Morristown, New Jersey: Silver Burdett, 1971.

Melodies for Music Makers. Far Rockaway, New York: Carl Van Roy Company, 1963.

New York Times Great Songs of the Sixties. Chicago: Quadrangle Books, 1970.

One in Song. Delaware, Ohio: Informal Music Service, 1965.

One Tune More. Delaware, Ohio: Cooperative Music Service. Revised, 1961.

Pocket Full of Songs. Delaware, Ohio: Informal Music Service, 1961.

Pointer System for Guitar. Winona, Minnesota: Hal Leonard Publishing Company, 1964.

Seventy-Two Giants. Miami Beach: Hansen Publishing Company.

Singing With Children. Belmont, California: Wadsworth Publishing Company, 2nd edition, 1970.

Sing Together Children. Delaware, Ohio: Cooperative Recreation Service. Revised, 1960.

Songs of Man. New York: Bonanza Books, 1965.

Travellin' On With the Weavers. New York: Harper and Row, 1966.

Work and Sing. Delaware, Ohio: Cooperative Recreation Service, 1948.

Appendix

MUSIC ACTIVITIES ADAPTED FOR CHILDREN
IN THE MAINSTREAMED CLASSROOM

Note: Most of the activities in this book can be done by all children. This Appendix lists those which have received special mention as being suitable for children with a specific handicap, or else represents those which suggest adaptations to make them suitable for children with handicaps.

Educable Mentally Retarded

Find High and Low Things—Chapter 1

Create Aleatory Melody or Mixed-Up Tunes—Chapter 2

Flash Cards—Chapter 2

Pin the Note on the Wall Staff—Chapter 2

Floor Staff Tag—Chapter 2

Who's on First Line—Chapter 2

Color Coding—Chapter 2

Play the Melody from the Notes—Chapter 2

Rearrange the Measures—Chapter 4

Pick a Rhythm—Chapter 4

Clap Three Kinds of Rhythm—Chapter 4

Play the Autoharp Using Color Coding—Chapter 6

Create Pentatonic Melodies Using Song Bells—Chapter 6

Mainstreaming and Classroom Instruments—Chapter 6

Mainstreaming, Music, and the Classroom Curriculum—Chapter 7

Have a Music Song Folder—Chapter 7

Motor Handicapped and Cerebral Palsied

Catch High and Low Balls—Chapter 1

Raise and Lower the Flag—Chapter 1

Ride the Waves—Chapter 1

Move Your Arms to the Sound of the Pitch—Chapter 1

Find Your Twin Note—Chapter 2

Stamp the Name—Chapter 3

Getting Fast and Getting Slow—Chapter 3

Play Freeze—Chapter 3

Play Two's, Three's, or Fours—Chapter 3

Step Rhythms and Change Places—Chapter 4

Have a Parade—Chapter 6

Hints Regarding Rhythm Activities for the Handicapped Child—Chapter 3

Mainstreaming and Classroom Instruments—Chapter 6

Partially Sighted

Hints Regarding Music Activities for the Handicapped Child—Chapter 3

Hard of Hearing

Play Mixed-Up Bells—Chapter 1

Pitch Notation Bingo—Chapter 2

Hints Regarding Rhythm Activities for the Handicapped Child—Chapter 3

Mainstreaming and Classroom Instruments—Chapter 6

Index